A LIFE IN TRANS ACTIVISM

A LIFE IN TRANS ACTIVISM

A. Revathi
As told in the original Tamil
and translated by Nandini Murali

zubaan

ZUBAAN
128 B Shahpur Jat, 1st Floor
NEW DELHI 110 049
Email: contact@zubaanbooks.com
Website: www.zubaanbooks.com

First published by Zubaan Publishers Pvt. Ltd 2016

10 9 8 7 6 5 4 3 2 1

ISBN 978 93 84757 75 5

Zubaan is an independent feminist publishing house based in New Delhi with a strong academic and general list. It was set up as an imprint of India's first feminist publishing house, Kali for Women, and carries forward Kali's tradition of publishing world quality books to high editorial and production standards. *Zubaan* means tongue, voice, language, speech in Hindustani. Zubaan publishes in the areas of the humanities and social sciences, as well as in fiction, general non-fiction, and books for children and young adults under its Young Zubaan imprint.

Printed at Raj Press, R 3 Inderpuri, New Delhi 110 012

•

To Famila, my daughter
and Deepu, my son

•

I did not have the good fortune to have children of
my own
I looked upon both of you as my children
You gave me the opportunity to experience
motherhood
As children you have to do the last rites for a mother
But you have made me do the last rites for both of you
How I suffer!
I dedicate this book to both of you
With deepest love and affection

Your amma
Revathi

Contents

REVATHI'S INTRODUCTION

Beyond Black and White

Breasts and long hair—is this a woman? Beard and moustache—is this a man? But what of the soul, which is neither man nor woman?

Devara Dasimayya, tenth century mystic and Kannada poet

Fear. I was scared to walk on the road for fear of people recognizing me. I was worried someone might mock me while I walked on the road. I was afraid the police might arrest me. I held back from taking the bus because I wasn't sure who I could sit next to. I was scared to use the public toilet for fear that people might know I was different. I was scared that rotten tomatoes might be thrown at me in the market. I was scared of falling in love for fear of being punished hard. Fear of everything and anything. Why am I so scared? This question haunted me.[1]

---

[1] Based on A. Revathi (2004): *Unarvum Uruvamum (The Feelings and the Body)* Revathi's first book, published in English and Hindi by Yoda Press, New Delhi.

Was I afraid because I knew my life would be difficult now that I had become a hijra? Because I was raised as a boy and now wore female clothes? Was it because of the way I lived—cast aside by parents, unrecognized by society, penalized by law and begging or doing sex work for a livelihood? What mistake had I made? Didn't my mother carry me for ten months like she did my siblings? Why did I have to suffer this fate? Why should I live in perennial fear all my life? Can't people understand how much I am suffering—I'm like the curd churned by the ladle or the worm burnt in the heat of the sun.

Is there a God at all, one who created us with male bodies but gave us female feelings? Are my parents responsible for this? Am I simply impudent to put on this garb? Who am I? Which gender do I belong to? Is it right or wrong to be like this? Where will I find answers to my questions?

In India, Ardhanareeswara, the half-male and half-female form of Shiva, is worshipped. Why then would such a country abuse hijras? How could those of you who have read the story of Shikandin in the *Mahabharatha* refuse to understand hijras? Are basic human rights meant only for males and females? Aren't hijras human enough to enjoy those rights? Aren't we citizens of this country? Don't we deserve to get voting rights, passports, driving licenses, ration cards and property rights? How justified is it to say that since I was born a male, I can get access to all these only if I remain a male? Don't I have the right to reassign my gender identity? Why do you refuse to understand me and my emotions?

I did not purchase these emotions; nor did I borrow them. I was made thus by nature. Respect that.

Recognize me as a woman and give me all the rights due to a woman. This plea for equality and human rights for transgender people has been the pivotal point of my transgender activism.

Myths and misconceptions about gender and sexuality have spread like poison in our society. We urgently need an antidote to this. I am a trans woman. This simply means that although I was seen as a male, even as a child I always felt that I was female. In India, we belong to the hijra community. In Tamil Nadu, we are known as Aravani or Thirunangai.

Several years back, I underwent surgical castration, sex change and hormone therapy to transition to womanhood. Since then, I have never looked back. But life as a woman has been a series of challenges. Even today, my greatest challenge is to live as a woman with respect and dignity.

People like me, whose experience of gender is different from what has been imposed on us at birth, face widespread stigma and discrimination. It begins in childhood because we are 'different' from the other children. For example, I loved to draw kolams, the beautiful floral and geometric rice flour designs women draw outside their homes in South India, to help my mother in the kitchen, I preferred to play with girls and to dress up as a girl. It seemed most 'natural' for me to do so. My family thought that this was just a passing phase. However, to their horror, when they realized that it was not, they began to punish me severely to make me behave like a 'normal' boy. At school, teachers and students made fun of me. I was called 'ombodu', 'ali' and 'pottai', all derogatory terms used to describe trans women and kothis.

Like me, every other hijra across caste goes through immense pain, sorrow, anguish, sexual violence and human rights violations. We are isolated and shunned by society.

For the past 17 years, I have been spearheading a campaign to address such issues through my role as a researcher and independent activist for the rights of gender minorities in south India. *Unarvum Uruvamum* was my first book. It was written in Tamil and later translated and published in English and Hindi. After the book was released, I attended a number of conferences in south India. I also met several ministers and VVIPs and gave them copies of the book in the hope that they would read it and do something for our transgender community. Unfortunately, as I realized later, they did not even open the book. But even if they did not, others did. Indeed, I feel humbled to acknowledge that some of the welcome developments related to gender and sexuality have sprung from my earlier book, *The Truth about Me* (2010),[2] which has currently been translated into seven Indian languages.

Today people ask us why the transgender community is involved in street based sex work and begging. They ask us why we can't do other work. But who will give us jobs? For instance, I don't get a consultation fee in universities where I'm invited to speak, although they pay for my travel when I am an invited speaker. Most members of the transgender community have low levels of education as we are thrown out of our homes and forced to discontinue

[2] A. Revathi (2010): *The Truth About Me*, New Delhi: Penguin India.

schooling. Then how can you tell us not to do sex work? What choice do we have?

It is now 69 years since India became independent. Despite the nearly seven decades, trans women like me, and trans men (people who are assigned female at birth but identify themselves as men) have not yet achieved full freedom. This is the truth. *The Truth about Me,* later published in Tamil as *Vellai Mozhi* (2010), has also been translated into Kannada, Malayalam and Telugu. These books have been stocked in libraries of more than 300 colleges and universities in the country. Together the books create awareness among students about gender and sexuality. As far as I know, the books form part of the prescribed syllabus in 20 universities and colleges.

The overwhelming public response for my books is a source of great satisfaction for me. I feel that the reason I took to writing has been validated. I can now see the fruit of my labour. It is a victory that is most meaningful for me. Ten years back, there was no such discussion among students about gender and sexuality. This was because of a general lack of awareness, and besides, there were not many books about the transgender community. The first autobiography to be written by a transgender person in India is Living Smile Vidya's *I am Vidya*. Originally written in Tamil, it has now been translated into English and several other Indian languages. *The Truth about Me,* an autobiographical account of my personal journey as a trans woman published in 2010, was an eye opener for the general public.

My life has been one long struggle to express and experience my identity as a woman. In my quest as a person born physiologically male, but who always desired to live as a woman, I experienced multiple oppressions from many sides—family, society, and in education, law, culture and caste. Although it has been uphill all the way, I emerged triumphant as a trans woman. There is no better teacher than one's lived experience. Today I speak frankly and fearlessly about the human rights violations, stigma, and discrimination and the rights of a trans woman to live like any other person.

In the last 17 years, I have been advocating for the rights not only of trans women but also of other gender and sexual minorities such as trans men, queers, gays, lesbians, bisexuals, kothis (trans people on the feminine end of the spectrum) and intersex individuals. Besides, as an activist, I support other marginalized communities such as dalits and adivasis. I am thankful that my voice is being heard through several spaces that are supportive of my activism. These include NGOs, colleges, universities, public meetings, media, theatre and writing.

The challenges, the triumphs and difficulties in my arduous journey as an activist form the core of this book. An unusual feature of this book is that it captures the narratives of trans men (female to male trans individuals), a highly invisiblized and marginalized gender minority. Most people are not even aware that such a group exists. And sadly, even most members of the hijra community do not accept them.

In 2012, supported by a one-year fellowship from Samvada, a Bengaluru-based youth sensitization and empowerment organization, I undertook a research project on female to male trans persons in South India. I had then resigned from Sangama, a Bengaluru-based organization for the rights of sexual and gender minorities, where I had been working for the past decade. However, I was unable to write my research based stories on trans men because by then, I had developed a nagging back problem. Conventional methods of treatment were not helpful. I did try to write, although my writing progress was slow.

I wanted the stories of the trans men to form an important part of this book. As a trans woman, I identify myself as a woman. Likewise, trans men identify themselves as men. I am a mother figure for many trans men.

I record my deepest gratitude for all the trans men who shared their stories with me with courage and honesty. The interview process itself was like that of a son sharing his story with his mother. As a staff member of Sangama, I was involved in the crisis interventions for a few of them when they came to Sangama. Hence to a large extent, I understood some of their issues and challenges. However, when I did the in-depth interviews with them, I literally lived their lives.

Unlike trans women, who have an alternative social support system such as the jamaat, and live together, trans men have no such support structures. These people find it nearly impossible to find a suitable female partner who accepts their identity as trans men. Thus their lives are at a crossroads and many do not know the best way forward. I want to take these young people along with me by leading the way just like a mother would. My deepest desire is that their stories should create awareness among parents, policy makers, professionals and the general public so that they are sensitive to their needs and concerns.

The different gender expressions which are physically manifested through clothing, body language, voice and other aspects of those who are born male but wish to live like females and vice versa, are ridiculed by society. At such times, I question the rigid categories such as male/female and feel that they are meaningless. Instead, I strongly believe that we need to go beyond male-female distinctions and learn to look at people as human beings.

Researching the lives of female to male trans persons has been a major milestone in my journey. Just as I identify as a woman and fight for women's rights, we also have to acknowledge trans men as men and respect their needs and concerns to live as men. Currently, my rights-based advocacy of trans men is a sadhana (a discipline) for me. While male to female trans persons go through intense struggles in their quest for womanhood, I feel the plight of trans men is, in many ways, worse. Their lives are shrouded in secrecy and silence, they go through far more intense stigma, discrimination and violation of human rights than so-called 'normal' people do. Even many professed feminist organizations, although aware of trans men issues, are not openly supportive of them.

If female to male trans persons are a reality, so also are male to female trans persons. Several people have told me that *The Truth about Me* opened their eyes to the truth that a transgender identity is as valid as any other and that there is nothing 'abnormal;' or 'deviant' about it. Among all the responses that poured in, there is one I cherish the most. After reading the book, a woman from Kerala, who is a teacher in a college, telephoned me. She said that the book had given her the courage and strength to be supportive of her daughter who, despite being biologically female, always identified herself as a boy/man. Today her daughter has transitioned to being male and is a very close friend of mine. As an adoptive mother to several female to male trans persons, I wish to tell the mothers of all such persons to wholeheartedly accept their children. If that happens, then this book would have served its purpose.

I cannot have biological children. But I have several children who are trans women and trans men. All of them call me 'Mummy'. When they do so, I experience the joy of actually having given birth to daughters and sons. In my 17 years of activism, I have also journeyed with my sons, have experienced their joys and sorrows, championed their causes and I continue to work for them. I have accepted them, the same way they have accepted me. Why then can't society accept them as sons and brothers? They are an inseparable part of my journey towards a world beyond borders and boundaries.

Although I had begun work on this book a while ago, my chronic back problem prevented me from writing regularly. At this point Dr Nandini Murali came into my life. Today when I look back, I can say that we were destined to meet. I shared with her my thoughts about the book. Nandini liked the idea and expressed her willingness to work on the book with me. Very soon, the book began to take shape.

And so I made several trips to Madurai, where Nandini lives. Together we began to breathe life into this book. Nandini visited me in Namakkal, where I live. Suddenly it seemed as if the distance between Namakkal and Madurai hardly mattered! During these trips, Nandini and I began to bond deeply with each other. That was hardly surprising because we spoke the same language—the language of inclusion and acceptance.

Nandini showers much love and affection on me. I often think we must have been sisters in a previous birth. I shared my story with her in Tamil. She recorded it and then translated it into English.

I want to express my heartfelt gratitude to her. But she tells me not to be so formal. She refuses to accept my gratitude because she considers me as a younger sister. According to her, between 'sisters', such formal thank yous are not necessary.

While in Madurai, I stayed in Nandini's home. I felt I was part of the family. I faced no discrimination. Initially even if I occasionally felt uncomfortable, she would reassure me and ensure that I was comfortable. Nandini's husband, Dr T.R. Murali, was equally supportive of my presence. Unlike many husbands, he did not cast aspersions on my character, and my community. He understood the seriousness of our work and ensured that it flowed along smoothly. Nandini, however, tells me that she would not have 'written' this book if she had been unable to throw open her home and heart to me. Her love and affection for me leaves me speechless. Truly, I am blessed to have her as my friend. Nandini's pet dog, Goldie, a beautiful Golden Retriever, also became fond of me. During my last visit, she was upset when I was leaving. Her angry barks, Nandini told me, conveyed her displeasure at my leaving the house. I was overwhelmed. If only human beings were as sensitive and caring!

At this point I must also mention that Nandini has requested Zubaan Publishers that her share of royalty should also go to me. Publicity-shy, she insisted that I must not mention this. But I've had bitter experiences of people who have exploited me commercially. And then there are others who pay lip service to inclusiveness and are just the opposite! But for every person who destroys my faith in humanity, there are people like Nandini, who restore my faith in the essential goodness of people by being genuine. Therefore I wish to make this publicly known.

In this connection, I must mention another interesting incident. A film-maker in Mumbai made a short film based on my book *The Truth about Me*. She invited me for the release. I got off the train in Mumbai at 4 am after a one and a half day journey. She invited me to her home. But once I went there, I realized many things. I had to change in the kitchen and wash my face in the waste storage area. I was made to feel an outcaste in every way. Worse, I got no credits or payment for the film! After the function she had me dropped me back at the station, just in time! I ran across the platform and jumped into the moving train!

Someone like this film-maker, who did not understand my feelings, what can she do for my community? She did the film for her personal name and fame. Nandini, on the contrary, treats me in a way that shows she respects me as a person and cares about my dignity. Our shared journeys—Nandini's and mine—will not stop with this book. The sisterhood will continue beyond the book. I shower a lot of love and affection on my family. But sadly they have not understood me at all.

The present book has been published by Zubaan Publishers, New Delhi. Urvashi Butalia, Publisher and Editor of Zubaan, released my earlier book, *The Truth about Me*, in 2010 in Delhi. She took the trouble to take the book for discussion to various fora and also invited me on some occasions. I am very fond of Urvashi. We have understood each other over the past five years. I am especially delighted that this book is being published by Zubaan. Penguin Books, which published the earlier book, also brought out the electronic and audio versions. For this and much more, I am thankful to Penguin.

I also thank the following organizations and people who were partners in this journey: Samvada, Sangama, LESBIT (a collective of Lesbians, Bisexual women, Intersex people and Transgender men), Dr Nandini Murali, Urvashi Butalia and the trans men I interviewed for this book.

A special thanks to my adopted son and trans activist Gee Imaan Semmalar, for his perceptive insights and editorial inputs, which have made a huge difference to the book.

I wish to thank film maker Satya Rai Nagpaul and Gee Imaan Semmalar for graciously permitting me to use their personal narratives in this book. I am immensely proud and grateful to all the trans men in this book—Kiran, Charu, Christy Raj, Mookan, Sonu Niranjan for sharing and trusting me with their stories. I also thank Eby, Deepu, Selvam, Sunil, Sreekanth for giving me interviews though their stories are not included in this book due to technical issues with the recordings.

My special thanks to M. Gopi Shankar, queer activist and founder, Shrishti Madurai, India's first registered LGBTIQ educational research centre, for his support.

To Sangama, where I had the opportunity to interact with several trans men and LESBIT, where I met a few trans men.

A well-known Tamil proverb says, 'Perform a marriage, beget a child, and construct a house'. What it implies is that each of these tasks is inherently difficult. For instance, a marriage should be within the same caste, community, religion, status, between man and woman, with the man older and taller! Dreams and hopes for a child begin at the moment of conception. Or perhaps even earlier. When it comes to building a house, we are advised to build it in a particular area, with vastu[3] specifications. But in any function associated with each of these momentous occasions, people start nit picking—they find fault with the food, arrangements and even the sex and physical features of the child.

In such a society, bound by numerous rules and regulations characteristic of a heteronormative, caste-based society, a child who changes from male to female or vice versa, is never accepted. Only those who have gone through the struggle know what it is to be gendered differently in a society that acknowledges imposed gender systems as natural and the norm.

There is no better teacher than lived experience. One should also have empathy and put oneself in the place of another person; see the world from that person's point of view. Unless that happens, we will only be looking at the world through a blinkered vision that sees the world in either black or white. And in doing so we miss the many shades of grey—which is what life is all about.

---

[3] Vastu is the ancient science of construction popularly found in Hindu architecture.

NANDINI'S INTRODUCTION

A Shared Sisterhood

When you meet a human being, the first distinction you make is, 'male or female?' and you are accustomed to make that distinction with unhesitating certainty.

—Sigmund Freud, *Femininity*

On a pleasant January morning in 2015, the plains of Tiruchnegode town sprawl as far as the eye can see. Situated here in Namakkal district in Tamil Nadu is the famous hill temple of Ardhanareeshwara. Revathi and I are seated in a small granite mandapam (temple porch) in the temple premises. The presiding deity in this 2000-year old temple is Shiva in the iconic form of Ardhanareeshwara, half-woman and half-man.

The temple was a most appropriate place to wrap up the marathon conversations between Revathi and I in the last six months. In retrospect, perhaps the place chose us. Because Revathi's life, both in letter and spirit, is all about transcending barriers and boundaries; narrow either-or definitions such as male/female, man/woman.

Revathi is a trans woman. As a child, when Revathi, then known as Doraiswamy, tried to live her 'growing sense of irrepressible femaleness', she was disowned by her family and excluded by society. But that's just one facet of this remarkable woman, who is also an author, poet, performer, and independent activist for the rights of differently gendered people, sexual minorities and an ally of other marginalized communities such as dalits and adivasis.

'There was never any confusion in my mind about my identity. I was always a woman. I was a woman then and am a woman now. I was in a man's body that I did not want. If you have six fingers instead of five, will you cut off all the fingers or you just get rid of the one finger you don't want? All I changed was the body that did not match. Yet over time, I realized that being a woman meant independence and assertion', Revathi once told me candidly.

I read Revathi's moving memoir, *The Truth about Me* (Penguin, 2010), when the magazine with which I was working, did a cover story on the transgender community in Tamil Nadu. I, however, met her for the first time last year when I was working on a study on the lives of the transgender community in the state. As I made my way to the sleepy hamlet near Namakkal where she lives, I was surprised to note that she was something of a celebrity in the village. Every person seemed to know her as they directed me to her residence with a sense of pride about the most famous resident of the village. From ostracism to a celebrityhood of sorts, Revathi's life has been a life lived perilously on the edge of a precipice.

Dressed in a maroon cotton sari with a beige border, the tall and statuesque Revathi greeted me with warmth and courtesy—something that comes naturally to her. Few women I know drape the sari better than Revathi. As we got talking, I realized that she was a person who spoke her mind fearlessly. Her rhetorical questions always had the same effect on me as a Zen master hitting his students to 'awaken' them to the present moment!

Even during our first meeting, it was obvious that Revathi exuded an intense presence. Although it was difficult to zero in on it, she embodied a certain idea of grace and courage.

During our conversation, Revathi wondered why sex work should not be considered as yet another form of work and was concerned that it was devalued and stigmatized. A former sex worker herself, Revathi makes no effort to minimize, erase, or disown that phase of her life. Candidly, she shared with me her intense dislike for the violation of bodily integrity she experienced as a sex worker. It was this violation—of body-mind-spirit—that made her give up sex work. A choice, she tells me, is intensely personal.

'Right now most transgender people are employed with NGOs. They are paid a small sum as salary, may be around ₹1500. And yet we tell them to give up sex work! How will they survive? I get annoyed when people tell us, "If we give your community alternative sources of employment, will you give up sex work?" Are we the only community to do so? Why hold us (transgender people) under the radar, and train a moral lens on us? After all, doesn't sex work happen everywhere? In massage parlours and in many such places clandestine sex work is common. I suppose we (transgender people) are singled out because we are visible,' says Revathi. She is convinced that sex work needs to be decriminalized.

The Truth about Me, Revathi's coming-of-age memoir, chronicles her struggles and agony as she negotiates the painful transition from Doraiswamy to her trans woman avatar as Revathi, through surgery and hormone therapy. Joining Sangama, a Bengaluru-based organization for the rights of sexual minorities and differently gendered people, Revathi tells me, was a turning point in her life. It led to her avatar as an activist, and this passionate activism informs who she is and why she does what she does today.

Seated in the serene and scenic ambience of the Ardhanareeshwara Temple, Revathi talks to me about her struggle to acquire a passport as a trans woman. In 2003, Revathi was all set to go to Dhaka, to participate as an invited speaker in an international conference, The South Asia Court of Women on the Violence of Trafficking and HIV/AIDS.

'Getting a passport was an affirmation of my rights as a citizen of India. But being a trans woman made it even more complex and difficult. There are only two boxes in the passport form: male or female. [This has now changed: NM] Besides it was impossible for trans people to provide address proof (as transgender individuals are a migrant community). We did not have ration cards, voter ID and bank accounts,' recalls Revathi.

However, armed with a letter from Sangama, the Bengaluru-based NGO where she was employed, and an affidavit provided by feminist activist Ashwini Sukthankar and her school-leaving certificate (that attested to her age), Revathi landed at the passport office in Bengaluru. To her dismay, the authorities pointed out the discrepancy in the name in her school-leaving certificate, which was Doraiswamy and her current name 'Revathi'.

'Although after my operation, I had legally changed my name to Revathi, it did not automatically mean that my gender was now female. There is no legal provision to do that. I told them that I am a trans woman who has undergone a sex change surgery. They insisted that I go to the doctor to get a medical certificate and literally drove me out,' recalls Revathi matter of factly.

Revathi was in a dilemma. Back in the early 1980s, a doctor who did surgical sex change did so stating that the penectomy (surgical removal of the penis, testes and scrotum) was being done due to cancer. No one was willing to give a medical certificate that the patient had undergone a sex change surgery. A desperate Revathi told the passport authorities that she could not trace the doctor. Not to be outdone, they instead asked her to get a medical certificate from an obstetrician and gynaecologist.

After repeated attempts, Revathi finally managed to get an appointment with a gynaecologist at a government hospital in Bengaluru. She said to him, 'I was born male but now after operation, am female. My problem is this: people call me "ombodu", "ali", "kattavandi", "duss", "pombalasatti", "khoja", "chakka", "mattuvandi", "double decker", etc. These are all derogatory Tamil terms that refer to effeminate traits and behaviour in boys and men. They're used to describe trans women. "Double decker" is sexual slang that refers to men who are sexually inclined towards men. I don't care if you give me a certificate as male or female. But give me one, please. I need to get a passport to represent my country at an international conference.

Am I a terrorist trying to fake a passport? As a doctor, it is your duty to examine me and give me a certificate,' she pleaded with the doctor, angry and helpless.

Listening to Revathi recount her struggles to get a passport—among the many things I take for granted—tears welled up in my eyes. Her pain and anguish were palpable.

Goaded by an insistent Revathi, the reluctant doctor finally decided to act. He ordered her to lift her clothes. He invited a group of nurses, ward boys, compounders and watchmen to watch him examine an 'unusual case'. They gathered around the examination table in voyeuristic delight as they gazed at a naked Revathi.

'The doctor examined my breasts and genital areas. The crowd around was smirking and many of them could hardly suppress their laughter. To them, I was a freak; an object of curiosity. But I put up with the humiliation because I wanted the passport. My life has been one long porattam (struggle) and there was so much I wanted to do for my community. If I had to face so much, won't the ordinary transgender who is so disempowered give up easily?' wonders Revathi in anguish.

Finally a triumphant Revathi got her passport as a female; making her the first trans woman in the country to do so. Revathi's life is, as she says, one long struggle, an uphill journey all the way. The challenges have been many. The first was the confusion, guilt and anxiety over her gender identity. Her family, like most families of differently gendered people, refused to accept that she did not wish to live like a male. Revathi writes poignantly about her brother's reaction to her cross-dressing and her feminine gendered preference in *The Truth about Me*.

> As soon as I reached home, my middle brother shut the door, grabbed a cricket bat and began hitting me, all the while screaming, 'That'll teach you to go with those Number 9s (a derogatory term for transgender people that means neither male nor female). Let's see you wear a sari or dance, you mother f****** *pottai!* He beat me hard mindlessly saying that he wanted to kill me. I tried to protect my face and head with my hands to keep the blows from falling. But they came down hard and I felt my hands swell. I was beaten on my hands and back and finally my brother brought the bat down heavily on my head. My skull cracked and there was blood all over, flowing warm.

Why are differently gendered people subject to such widespread stigma and discriminatory practices in society? Why do transgender individuals evoke such fear, ridicule and hatred in society?

Transgender is an umbrella term that includes a range of people with diverse gender identities and experiences. It includes kothis or pre-operated trans people at the feminine end of the spectrum, post-operative transgender women, and non-operated transgender people (both of whom identify with the gender that is diametrically the opposite of their biological sex), and other gender non-conforming individuals. A male to female transgender person is referred to as a trans woman, and a female to male transgender as a trans man.

Revathi told me, 'It's not that we are arrogant and cut off our balls because we have nothing else to do or becausewe are crazy!' Until she put it so bluntly,

I hadn't realized that this tendency to identify with a gender that is opposite to a person's biological sex is now described as Childhood Gender Nonconformity (CGN). Biological sex is determined at birth by chromosomes and the presence of sex organs.

'One is not born, but becomes a woman,' said Simone de Beauvoir, the French feminist philosopher. While sex is a biological fact, gender identity, the process of becoming a man or woman, is socio-culturally constructed based on traditional masculine and feminine stereotypes associated with being male and female respectively. Gender identity refers to a person's deep-seated feelings of whether one is a boy/girl, man/woman. In other words, it is one's *feelings*, and not one's biological sex that determines gender identity.

During our several conversations, Revathi reiterated that gender is not determined by the genitals or as she memorably said, 'by what is (or not) between your legs and chest!' Rather, she reminded me that gender identity refers to the innermost feeling of 'who I actually am. I am a woman or man because I feel like one; not because of the sex organs!'

'I am a man or I am a woman' is how usually a person identifies with or feels himself or herself to be. For most people, there is a match or congruence between one's anatomical sex and gender identity. For a minority, however there is a mismatch, between the anatomical sex and gender identity. This is termed gender incongruence, or transgenderism. This mismatch and the resulting feelings of confusion, loneliness, anxiety, guilt and shame are termed gender dysphoria. Significantly, the American Psychiatric Association (APA) in 2012 declassified transgenderism from being described as a disorder and replaced it with the term gender dysphoria.

The concept of a gender binary[1] or gender binarism helps us understand the social exclusion and vulnerabilities experienced by transgender individuals. The gender binary helps us to understand the widespread stigma, discrimination and multiple oppressions experienced by gender variant individuals who do not fit into the rigid either-or (male/ female) binary gender categories. The term gender binary describes a societal worldview that splits people into opposing male and female, sex and gender, masculine and feminine—all of which are seen as hierarchical, opposing and disconnected. And most importantly, generally, the male is overvalued vis a vis the female. Associated with this, however, are factors such as caste and class.

The gender binary splits and compartmentalizes people into male and female gender roles, gender identities and attributes. In this rigid map of what it means to be male-female, man/woman, people who are gender diverse—whose gender identity, gender experience and biological sex do not 'match' or align with social norms, are marginalized and thereby excluded because they do not conform to normative gender expectations associated with one's biological sex.

Genderism,[2] or the belief that there are only two genders and that gender is inherently associated with one's assigned sex at birth, is the basis of the

[1] http://en.wikipedia.org/wiki/Gender_binary, https://www.genderspectrum.org/understanding-gender, both accessed on December 5, 2014
[2] Ibid.

pervasive trans phobia or the widespread fear, hatred and avoidance of people such as transgender persons.

The Truth about Me: A Hijra Life Story is a powerful narrative that traces the trajectory of Revathi's transformation from a biologically male Doraiswamy to her status as Revathi, a trans woman. Finally she is able to achieve the deeply desired congruence between her anatomical sex and her gender identity. The narrative talks about Revathi's intense struggles to acquire a transgender identity. At a crossroads now, she finds herself confronted by several new challenges. 'I am a transgender who wishes to live like a woman,' says Revathi, who acknowledges it as her source of joy and pain.

In this book Revathi dwells on her sustained activism for the rights of sexual minorities, particularly the transgender community that has defined her work from 2000 onwards. The narrative dwells on the realities and complexities of the lives of the transgender community. A unique feature of Revathi's trans activism is her passionate plea that the needs and concerns of trans men or female to male trans people, be highlighted on par with those of trans women. A rights-based approach (rather than the conventional welfare approach that hands out mere sops to people traditionally regarded as objects of pity), is the thematic motif that knits this narrative.

This book unfolded as a series of long conversations—spread over six months—between Revathi and me. We spoke in Tamil, our first language. I was pleasantly surprised to discover that ambiguities and equivocations, often the nightmare of a translator, were non-existent for me! Perhaps we spoke the same language; of inclusiveness. I also think that it was because Revathi was clear and precise in what she wanted to convey.

There were times Revathi visited me in Madurai, where I live. And I visited her at Namakkal, where she lives. Every time Revathi visited me, I was touched by her thoughtful gifts of fruit and sweets, both of which are my favourites. During our conversations, we discovered that despite our differences, we were so similar as women and in our quest for womanhood: although each of us experienced it differently, as feminists, as writers, and as seekers on a quest for personhood

We gradually developed a bond that I can only describe as a sisterhood. Revathi modelled for me a homespun brand of feminism; native and anchored in the realities of our country. It was feminism shorn of every trace of rhetoric and pretence; a feminism that embraced plurality and diversity as it strove for equality and inclusion—not only for differently gendered people but also other marginalized communities such as adivasis, dalits and people with mental and physical challenges.

Working on this book with Revathi has been an inward journey for me. Slowly but persistently she shone the light of honesty and truth that enabled me to excavate and bring to the surface my own deeply embedded fears, prejudices and biases... the pairs of opposites that paradoxically melted and dissolved in the light of truth. For this and for her abiding friendship and sisterhood, I am happy that our paths crossed.

What follows is Revathi's story—the story of a resilient woman who decides to live life on her own terms—as a trans woman, with dignity and courage. In the narrative of her life, Revathi weaves the story of human rights, of the political, the ethical and the aesthetic warp and weft of the trans community into a narrative of hope and triumph.

Interacting with Revathi has enabled me to confront the true meaning of difference, diversity, tolerance and acceptance. Diversity is the law of nature. Imagine, a monocultural world—how lifeless and colourless it would be! However, while differences give rise to diversity; hierarchies are a human construct. It is all too easy for us to say that we are accepting of differently gendered people, when in reality it is just tolerance. True acceptance springs from actively engaging with the Other; to seek to enlarge our interface; to build bridges of understanding through a process of dialogue; to embrace the Other so that there is only the Self.

How then do we actively engage with plurality and diversity and thereby promote pluralism? Diana Eck in *Encountering God: A spiritual journey from Bozeman to Benares,* writes that pluralism is something more than just tolerance. Pluralism protects and nourishes diversity.

> Tolerance can enable coexistence, but it is certainly no way to be good neighbours. Tolerance does not take us far with ideas that challenge our own. Tolerance, is of course, a step forward from active hostility. Tolerance alone does nothing to improve our ignorance of one another by building bridges of exchange and dialogue. Tolerance does not require us to know anything new. It might sustain a temporary and shaky truce, but it will never bring forth a new creation.

Engaging with the world of trans people and placing their personal narratives in the public domain has helped me to push my personal boundaries and gain fresh insights into the meaning of pluralism and why we need to promote pluralism by dialogue and understanding. Pluralism is the receptive ocean into which all rivers of difference dissolve and merge. After all, the ocean refuses no river. I hope that Revathi's story inspires many of us to increase our bandwidth to accommodate and truly accept differences and diversities.

Revathi reminds me of a lotus in full bloom. Her incredible story is one of courage, optimism and faith. It is mired in societal prejudices, biases, fears, oppression and a desire to homogenize all differences. Such is the substratum in which Revathi's life is anchored. Like the lotus, her life is one upward burst of aspiration and glory. The lotus, as we all know, blooms only when mired in a swamp.

PS: I wish to acknowledge Dr T.R. Murali, my spouse, for having created the space for me to pursue my literary aspirations; and Goldie, our gorgeous Golden Retriever, for being my soulmate, incredible companion and foot warmer, all rolled in one! Goldie was always by our side when Revathi and I were working together on this book. She died recently and I wish she had been alive to see the book published.

1

Biology is Not Destiny

Who am I? This was a question I often asked myself even as a child. I know it is not common for children to ask such questions. But then I was no ordinary child. I don't mean that I was exceptional in any way, but I certainly was 'different' from most children.

I was born on April 14, 1968, in a small village near Namakkal, a town near Salem in Tamil Nadu. The name Namakkal comes from the Tamil word Namagiri, which is the name of the single rock formation in the centre of the town. Namakkal is famous for its cave-cut Narasimha Perumal (one of the ten avatars of Vishnu) and Namagiri Thayar (the goddess Lakshmi) temple, the towering Anjaneya Temple, the Mariamman and Vinayaka temples, all of which are in the heart of the town. There is also the famous hill fort, which is actually a temple carved out of a single rock. A high wall built during the time of Tipu Sultan, surrounds the fort. Every year, during the month of Panguni (mid-March to mid-April), in the Tamil calendar, a ten-day temple festival takes place.

Traditionally agriculture is the main occupation of the people of this region. Today, the town is famous for its educational institutions, poultry, lorries and workshops that build 'bodies' for heavy vehicles.

My family consisted of my parents and five siblings. We were four brothers and a sister. I am the youngest. Being the youngest, my parents and siblings pampered and showered their love and affection on me. They named me Doraiswamy.

My father and my eldest brother were in the milk vending business. My father drove a lorry that transported milk collected from the nearby villages and delivered it to the milk factory. It was a difficult life. They began their day at 4 am every day and milk had to be delivered by 9.30 am on the same day. In case the lorry broke down and they delivered the milk late, or the milk turned sour, because of the delay, they earned that much less that day.

***

Ever since I can remember, I always helped my mother with housework such as cooking, cleaning, sweeping, swabbing and washing vessels. I swept the entrance of our home every morning, splashed water, and made elaborate kolam, which in South India is a traditional art form—making decorative patterns with rice flour—and is always practised by women and girls.

I went to the government school for boys in the village. I walked to the school along with the girls from the neighbourhood. When I was five years old, like most children of that age, I played together with boys and girls. We even peed together! At that time we had no rigid distinctions such as 'You are a girl!' and 'I am a boy!' Isn't it strange and even sad that only as we grow older do we acquire the notion that the two sexes are very 'different' and therefore we should stay apart from one another?

When I was growing up, I noticed that girls had many restrictions. So many dos and don'ts were imposed on them. They were constantly being told to behave like 'good' girls, be modest, talk softly and not to play with boys! And I also noticed that boys had a lot of freedom and did not have to live by such rules and regulations.

The only restriction I faced was that when I was in Class 7, the boys were told not to play with girls. Yet all the time I wanted to be with them and play with them. Although I was physiologically a boy, psychologically, I felt I was certainly a girl. I even peed squatting like a girl. In fact I was hesitant to pee with the boys, because I always felt that I *am* a girl! Even then I often wondered why society boxes people into rigid compartments of boy vs. girl.

Often, when I got back from school, I'd play a little game. I'd put on my sister's long skirt and blouse, twist my hair into a towel and let it trail down my back like a braid. I would then pretend I was a shy bride, my eyes downcast, and my family would laugh. Since I was very young, it was a source of great amusement and entertainment for them and no one gave it much thought. 'He is a small child. He will outgrow it,' they said.

Because I was often found in the company of girls, people began to openly make fun of me. They began to call me derogatory names such as 'ombodhu' (Number 9), 'ali', 'pottai' and 'pombalasatti' (female thing). Some even teased me, 'Are you a boy? Why do you walk like a girl? Why do you wear girl's clothes?'

I had no ready retorts to their teasing. I knew deep down that I *am* indeed a girl. In fact that is what I wanted to be. Ironically, when I was young, even such name-calling was a source of secret pride and happiness for me as I realized that they were indirectly acknowledging my latent femaleness. Later, however, as I grew older, it became a source of pain, shame and humiliation.

At school, the boys played gilli-danda, football, cricket and cops and robbers but these games had no interest for me. I played with the girls—five stones, paandi (hopscotch) and hide and seek. Even the girls often said to me, 'Poda! Why do you play with us? Go play with boys!'

I always told them that I felt happier being with them. But sadly, as I grew older, even the girls were embarrassed by me and did not want to include me in their group. I thought to myself that it is strange that when children are young, they run around naked, play and even pee and shit together. Where are the boy-girl differences in childhood?

I often looked at girls, noticing the way their plaits fell, their skirts and blouses, the intricate knots of their colourful ribbons, the malli (jasmine) and kanakambaram (firecracker flowers) in their hair. That I was 'different' from the other boys was obvious to teachers and students in school. They openly began to tease me.

My teachers punished me because I spoke like a girl and my body language was feminine. They even caned me becaue they said I was not brave like boys should be. And because I did not play boys' games, the PT (physical training) master punished me. He once said to me, 'Are you a girl or what? Pull your trousers down! Let me check!' He mock stripped me and I began to cry. But everyone just laughed.

My feminine behaviour made me vulnerable in other ways as well. When I was in Class 7, a teacher fondled me and pinched me on the cheeks, chest and thighs. He did not do this to the other boys. Although I was too young to understand then that this was child sexual abuse, today I understand that because of my femininity, despite being physiologically male, I was as vulnerable to sexual exploitation as a girl child. So it's not only girls but also children who are born male who identify themselves or express their gender as female, who are victims of sexual exploitation.

When I was in Class 7, I experienced my first sexual attraction. I fell in love with a boy. I was confused. Was this right or wrong? I was troubled by guilt and anxiety. To make matters worse, I could not share this with anyone. I could not openly express my feelings, my desires and longings. Society has such rigid definitions of what it means to be a boy or girl and expectations of appropriate behaviour for a boy/man, girl/woman. We have drawn a rigid closed circle around ourselves and we live in this prison of our own making.

Under such circumstances, had I been a girl who was sexually or romantically attracted towards a boy, at least I could have openly expressed my feelings. Because I was a boy, I felt inhibited to express my love for another boy openly. Ironically, although I was unable to be open about my love, I had a few opportunities to express my femininity openly.

***

One such opportunity was when I played the role of Chandramathi in a school play, *Harishchandra*. For my particular scene, I had to walk to a sad song, my false hair streaming around me and the sari end held out like a begging bowl. My friends declared that I was not acting, but that I literally lived the role of Chandramathi! Yet I was sad that I could express myself only in such indirect ways. Would it possible for me to behave openly like this? Could I go to school dressed like a girl? Could I be like one in my family? Could I fetch water for my mother, chop vegetables and do all the household chores as girls did?

At the same time I often wondered if such desires were 'wrong' or 'sinful'. Is this a disease? Am I the only one who has such feelings? Or are there others like me? If so, how and where would I find them? I was angry with God. Why did he make me a male but give me the feelings of a female? There was no one I could share my feelings with. I felt alone and lonely.

As a result I was unable to concentrate on my studies and it began to reflect in my performance at school. I frequently absented myself from school. I cut classes, and watched Tamil films with money stolen from my father's shirt pocket. I loved watching MGR and Saroja Devi films. When I was inside the theatre for two and half hours, I forgot all my troubles. But they engulfed me again when I came out. One day, I dressed up like Saroja Devi and was even acting like her. I was lost in the performance. When my mother saw me, she complained to my father and brothers. I have described this painful incident in *The Truth About Me*:

They had a plan for me. First, they thrashed me soundly. 'You mother-fucking sissy! So young and yet you steal money to go to the cinema? Can't you see that we are working only to send you to school? You had better make sure that you go to school! From now on, first thing in the morning, you will gather all the buffalo dung there is, feed the animals, water them and then leave for school. You'll do this in the evening too, as soon as you return home. Only then you'll know what life is, how tough it is.'

How could I expect them to know what I was going through? I bundled my feelings and confusions into a tight ball, laid them aside, and in spite of all the teasing and bullying, went about doing what I was asked to do. This lasted for some time.

***

The annual festival at the Mariamman Temple in our village is a grand event. Every evening, during the ten-day long festival, plays would be staged. I never missed even a single one. One day, a group of boys from the village asked me if I would like to dress up as a kurathi (female gypsy) and go around the neighbourhood singing, dancing and collecting money for the temple, since I anyway appeared feminine. Although I liked the idea, I was afraid my brothers would find out and hell would break loose. But the others convinced me that I was doing it for the sake of the goddess.

To the world it must have seemed that I was playing a woman, but inside, I felt I *was* a woman. I had to make my chest big and so wore a blouse stuffed with cloth balls. I had on a skirt, anklets, a long braid of false hair adorned with paper flowers. My eyes were lined with kohl and my lips painted red. I knew I looked beautiful. I looked at myself in the mirror several times and was astonished to see what I had become.

The boy who had to play my partner said, 'Hey, Doraiswamy! You look like a real woman. If you were one, I'd fall in love with you!'

I blushed. Although the other boys sniggered, I felt wonderful. As we walked, people wondered, 'Hey! Who is this kurathi? Is she a real woman or a dressed up one?'

As we began dancing, a few men got close to me and said, 'What have you got there? Coconut shells?' Irritated, I pushed their hands away. The crowd roared with laughter. Although I was enjoying the performance, I was afraid of my brothers.

By the time I went home, everyone—including my family—knew that I was the kurathi. My mother fumed, 'OK, so you dressed up? But why dress up as a girl? Don't you have any shame?'

But as I insisted that I had done it for the goddess, my family let me off the hook. And the entire village was all praise for me. A few people said that I ought to have been born a woman and that it was unfortunate that I had been born a man. In my kurathi garb, I could express all those female feelings I usually had to suppress and felt so happy for days afterwards. But I was troubled by the feelings men evoked in me.

Would I be able to find somebody who felt the way I did? Not surprisingly, I failed my Class 10 examinations. Around this time I met a person who told me that there were people in a place nearby who were born as men and changed themselves into women. This place was the hill fortress in Namakkal. When I went there I was amazed to discover that there were indeed many people like me. These men wore their lungis like saris and walked as if they were women. These effeminate boys and men spoke to me with a lot of love and affection. We addressed each other as 'Vaa di! Podi!' which is a Tamil endearment used by women for their women friends. This I felt to be the language of feminine friendship and intimacy. When we began to talk, we realized that all of us were raised as boys but wished to live like women.

I wanted to become like them. They told me that if I wanted to become a woman, I should go to Bombay or Delhi where I could live independently as I wished. I was scared but decided to go because I felt I was a woman and wanted to run away from my family and society who did not accept me as I am.

***

I began to visit the hill fortress often to meet my friends and be myself; unafraid of ridicule or being hurt. I sang and danced and spent several happy hours with people who were like me and with whom I could be myself. At this point I must stress that no child wants to run away from home. But when a (gender non-conforming) child like me begins to seek others like him or her, it is because there is no one in the family who is supportive. I don't blame my family either. They were ignorant about such things.

When a child is growing into adolescence, he or she has so many needs. For instance, it's at this point in life that children begin to experience sexual attraction. We feel the need to gaze at a boy or a girl. In Tamil we colloquially refer to this as 'sight adikiradhu!' This is a harmless pastime and is often just fantasy.

But it is important for the adolescent. However, even heterosexuals have difficulty talking about love and romance to others. Imagine then our plight!

But if I want to gaze at a boy or man, I cannot do it openly. This is why I was forced to seek out someone who shared my feelings. I needed to look for such people. Naturally, when I began to do so, I did not tell to my family what I was doing or who I was meeting. So they began to get suspicious of me. They wanted to curb my freedom. They often thrashed me, hoping to 'correct' what they perceived as my feminine behaviour.

***

'You mother-fucking sissy! We know all along that you have been roaming around the village like an ombodhu! Have you ever thought what people will say about our family? What is it you lack here? Don't you have enough to eat and good clothes to wear? Your brothers labour in grease and grime as lorry drivers. We have high hopes that you will be educated and get a decent job. And you do this to us!' This from my brother as he beat me within an inch of my life.

My friends at the Namakkal hill fortress once told me about a group of men who had turned into women. These people, who lived in Bombay and Delhi, came every year to Dindugul, for the annual Mariamman festival. They stayed with a senior person, Xavieramma. I wanted to meet them. So I used some of my tuition money to buy bangles, ribbons and earrings. I also took my sister's skirt, blouse and half-sari. When I went there, I was told that all these men had undergone castration and and they were known as hijras. This was the first time I heard the word. I couldn't believe my eyes when I saw them—everyone looked so feminine! Only their voices gave them away. As soon as they saw us, they knew what we were all about.

'Come, bete! Where are all of you from? Say Paampaduthi (a traditional greeting in the hijra community) to your elders,' they instructed us. As my friends touched their feet and said 'Paampaduthi, amma', I did the same. As soon as we did this, the sari-clad elders said, 'Jiyo! Jiyo!' I soon learnt how important it was that a feminine kothi offers respect to the sari-clad hijras and earns their goodwill. I soon learnt that this is part of the hijra tradition.

We participated in the Molapari or ritual offering of germinated seeds to the goddess Mariamman where we walked to the temple carrying pots of seedlings on our heads. For the first time, I wore a sari, wig, braided false hair, bangles and earrings and nose rings. I was around 14 or 15 years old at the time. I was tall and slim and had no facial hair, and no hair on my arms and legs.

Several members of the community congratulated me and exclaimed, 'Amma! She looks like a real woman and so beautiful! If you undergo nirvaanam (castration) you will become just like us! See, she looks like the actress Revathi!'

I was delighted to be compared to Revathi, a popular Tamil film heroine of the 1980s. And in my heart, I imagined that was my name—Revathi. I looked at myself in the mirror and felt a glow of pride. I did look like a woman. It was at that moment I discovered that I was indeed one.

I wanted to undergo castration immediately because I so wished to live like a woman. But the hijras told me that it is not so easy. To get the operation done, I had to become a chela (disciple or daughter) to a senior hijra, who is known as a guru in the hijra tradition. I had to live with my guru for two years, take care of her, earn for her and once I had understood the hijra culture and tradition, then my guru would help me with the surgery..

I requested the hijra elder to accept me as her chela. She said, 'Our jamaat meets tomorrow evening. I will accept you as a chela tomorrow evening in front of the jamaat.'

The hijra jamaat is a collective of transgender people. For people like us, who are forced to leave our homes because our families refuse to accept our gender identity as women, the jamaat offers us shelter and protection. It is a sanctuary.

That evening when the jamaat elders met, all of us sat in a circle around a plate, on which was spread a white cloth. On it were placed some betel leaves and a rupee and twenty five paise. My guru announced that she would like to adopt me as her chela and for this, she was willing to give five rupees and also one rupee and twenty five paise to the jamaat. The latter is known as thandu (fee) money. The others received the thandu money in my guru's name and placed it on the plate. They took the five-rupee note and noted that this was 'for Revathi' and muttered, 'Five Rupees for Revathi, *deen deen*!' The others then showed their appreciation by clapping and shouting.

From then on, I had to address my guru as I would address my mother—Amma. My guru in turn announced that she was my mother and that my name was Revathi. She asked me to do paampaduthi to all elders. I did so and my guru hugged and kissed me and ran her fingers through my hair.

Meanwhile my guru had to leave the next day for Delhi. I did not want to go back home as I was afraid that my brothers would want to know where I had been and would then beat me up. So along with some of my friends I found refuge in a hijra community in Erode, about 50 kms from my home town. Here I met many more people who had undergone castration and who dressed like women. They danced the Karagattam, a Tamil folk dance performed during temple festivals. They also made periodic visits to Bombay and Delhi to visit the hijra communities in the two cities.

**

I desperately wanted to become a woman, to become like them. I asked if I too could wear a sari. How long would it take for my hair to grow to the right length? They said that I needed to grow my hair and get my nose and ears pierced before I wore a sari. I found out why they insisted on such things. If I wore a sari without having grown my hair, I would be a man wearing a sari and that was a dishonour for the entire hijra community.

When I heard this I wept because it meant that until I managed to grow my hair, I would have to dress like a man. I also learnt that while we felt like women, it was equally important to look like them and therefore the long hair was an important marker of being feminine. I did whatever work the hijras gave me. Often it involved a lot of domestic work such as cooking, cleaning, washing, sweeping and swabbing and fetching water. I was told that all of us pottais (pre-operated transgender) had to go through this difficult phase if we wanted to undergo castration. I also learnt to cook and dance. My nani (my guru's guru) in Erode had a folk dance troupe and we performed regularly at temple festivals.

***

It was almost a month since I had left home. My sister's wedding was to take place soon and I badly wanted to attend. So I took a bus to Namakkal. My mother wept on seeing me. But my elder brother was furious.

'What happened to you? Are you mad to run away without informing us? We have been searching for you all over!' He yelled as he hit me with a cricket bat. I muttered that I had been to Madurai with a friend from the tuition class and retuned in time for Akka's (elder sister) wedding. Since the wedding was to happen soon, I got off with this excuse. But my brother was disgusted that I had long hair.

After the wedding, my brothers and father ordered me to work as a cleaner in the lorry the family owned. They scolded me in front of the workers and humiliated me. I was forced to do all the difficult jobs that men usually did. My father was always unhappy with me, no matter how hard I worked.

'You'll learn only by drinking their piss,' he sneered as he pointed to the others.

This was too much for me. I could not bear the insults, thrashings and scolding any more. The instant he shouted, I decided to leave home once again, perhaps never to return. Soon after, I stole one of my mother's earrings and taking two of her saris with me, boarded the train to Delhi.

***

In Delhi, I lived in the house of a hijra in Wazirpur. I dressed like a woman and had my ears and nose pierced. A hijra elder adopted me as her daughter and I accompanied her when she visited the shops, begging for money. I did not like doing this. But I accompanied her, only because I had no other option. I also accompanied other hijras. There were many groups of hijras living in our neighbourhood and all of us went around begging. At the end of the day, we would share our earnings. I wasn't given any money as my share went directly to the hijra in whose house I stayed. I also did all the domestic chores in her house.

Initially, I did not mind doing all the work. But later, it became difficult, as I had to wash all the vessels in which the senior hijras had spat. They told me not to make a fuss about washing their spit because as youngsters they too had done it for the elders. They also told me that I should consider myself fortunate to serve the elders. Doing so, they reassured me, would bring me good luck and enable me go through nirvana quickly. I lived in these difficult circumstances for about three to four months. My only happiness was that my hair had grown to shoulder length by then.

Meanwhile, my family had found out that I was living as a hijra in Delhi and that I begged for alms to make a living. I decided to return home when I heard that my mother was seriously ill. I took off my hijra clothes at Salem railway station and went home dressed in male clothes. I was fearful that my mother's health would worsen if she saw me dressed in a sari. I wondered what explanation to give my family this time.

I got home around 9 in the morning. I found, to my relief, that my mother was perfectly well.

My middle brother was home. The moment he saw me, he closed the door and began to hit me with a cricket bat. 'That'll teach you to go with those ombodhus! Let's see you wear a sari again or dance, you mother-fucking pottai!' I thought I would die, that he would never stop. I tried to protect myself but he kept shouting and raining blows on me. I felt my hands swell up. He beat me on my legs, back, and finally, he brought the bat down heavily on my head. My skull cracked and there was blood all over, flowing, warm.

'That's right! Beat him and break his bones. Only then will he stay at home and not run away!' I heard my mother say.

I finally managed to push my brother away and ran into a room and locked the door. It seemed to me then that it was better to take my own life than let my brother beat me to death. I was looking around to see if there was something I could use, when my brother broke open the door and came after me again. He hit me again, till he was tired and his arms ached and when he was exhausted, he stopped.

'Why don't you understand my feelings? Why do you hit me even before you ask me anything? I am here only because of the love I have for all of you. What have I done that you should beat me so?'

My brother told me that he had heard that I had been spotted in women's clothes begging along with a few other pottais in the market. The local pottais were taken off to the police station where they confessed that I was in Delhi.

'How can you do this to us? What have we not done for you? Have you lacked for anything? Why do you have to join a gang of pottais, wear saris and beg? How can someone from a good family do this? How can you forget all this and do what you did?' asked my mother in anger and sorrow.

Unable to bear the pain, I confessed that I had been lured away to Delhi. That stopped the beating. But my family decided to shave off my hair. My mother said, 'Tomorrow we will go to the Samayapuram temple and there he can offer the hair to the goddess. She will help cure him and soon he will be free from mohini pisasu (seductive female demon) who even now has a hold on him.'

***

The next day when my hair was shorn off at the temple, I felt more pain and hurt at this than when my brother thrashed me. I wanted to pour out my sorrow in front of the goddess. But even that I had to do silently. Within myself. I felt like an ocean churning. But I had to keep my feelings bottled up.

I silently asked the goddess, 'Amma! Why am I suffering like this? What have I done wrong? It was you who made me in male form, but with female feelings. Now I am being punished and in your own shrine! Aren't you a woman too? Can't you understand another woman's feelings? By this time next year, please make me a woman, just like you. If you can't, at least make me into a man, completely.'

My head was now completely shaven. I shut myself up at home. I was the object of pity and curiosity. They say that only those who have experienced hurt and pain will know the pain of others and so it was for me. How could I expect these people to understand how my body and mind were bruised?

I had to wait for my hair to grow before I took off to Delhi again, for a person with a shaven head has no standing among pottais. In three months time, I left for Delhi again. In Delhi, my guru decided that I should go to Mumbai. My hair was short and I had not had the surgery. It was not easy to live like that in Delhi and I would therefore be a dishonour to the hijra community. Besides, my family would know of my whereabouts.

***

Accompanied by another hijra, I boarded the train for Mumbai. My guru told me that I had to stay there till my hair grew back and I had my operation, after which she would take me back. In Mumbai, I joined a hijra community in Vikhroli near Ghatkopar. It was here that I learnt all about the hijra way of life, its culture, customs and traditions. I learnt of relationships within the community such as those between the guru (teacher) and chela (disciple), and nani (maternal grandmother). The hijra community has seven gharanas or houses. Each house has its own nayak or leader. To become somebody's chela, it is necessary to bring the seven nayaks together in a jamaat (the social support system in the hijra community) and place a reeth (a symbolic token of adoption) in their presence.

I learnt that I could become a chela of another guru if I was dissatisfied with my present guru. I also became aware of other 'rules' of the community: you never cut your hair, you always touch the feet of elders at the beginning and end of the day and you need to be careful about your clothes coming in contact with those of the elders.

I was asked to go to the shops every day and beg for money. I also did all the domestic work. Six months passed this way. Although life was tough, I was happy that I was living like a woman. Around this time, my guru decided that I was ready for the nirvana ceremony and sent me to Dindugul, a small town in Tamil Nadu, where the procedure was performed for the hijra community.

My nani asked me, 'Do you want to have your surgery done by a thayamma or a doctor?' A thayamma operation is performed by a hijra on someone who aspires to be a hijra. An operation by a doctor takes place in a hospital. Although I did not fully understand the implications of nani's question, I was thrilled. I wanted to jump up and down in excitement. I was afraid that if I hesitated she might not send me. So I told her that it was up to her to send me wherever she wished.

***

Deep inside my heart, I was afraid of the thayammma operation. But I also knew that those who had this operation were considered special in the community. But more than anything, I was eager to become a woman and that was all that mattered to me. At that time, I believed that if I wanted to become a woman, all that I needed to do was to get rid of the male organ. The sight of it disgusted me. I was ready to even chop it off myself.

'You may not be able to bear a thayamma operation. It is best you get it done by a doctor,' said nani.

Accompanied by another hijra who also was to undergo the procedure, we left for Dindugul. Before the operation, the doctor gave me an injection in my lower back. He said it would make me numb below the hip and I would not feel any pain during the operation. The nurse covered my eyes with a strip of cloth, and asked me to say, 'Mata, Mata!' and I did so. I kept repeating the name of the goddess. The doctor continued to do his work. Although I could not see anything, I heard the sound of the knife scraping.

'Do you want me to arrange things so that you pee like women do, from below?' asked the doctor, 'or as men do from above?'

'I want to live as a woman, which is why I wanted this operation. Please make it like it is for a woman.' I did not know how women peed, but I wanted to be a woman. The operation took two hours. Afterwards, the doctor brought me a cup with pieces of flesh in it.

'Here! Look at what's left of your organ. We cut it off and made a woman out of you.'

I was ecstatic. At last I was a woman. But the pain after the effect of anaesthesia had worn off was unbearable. I wonder how I survived that agony. On the sixth day, the doctor removed my stitches. Peeing and shitting were terribly painful. In those days, there were no nighties, so we held our saris high, away from the area that had been operated on, and walked with our legs apart. If the pee did not flow freely, we had to be careful not to force it out, for it would hurt unbearably and bleed. As for shitting, I had to take a deep breath to force things out as I felt my nerves would snap. Oh! The things I had to put up with in order to become a woman!

My nani gave ₹7000 to my hijra friend and I, of which ₹5000 was for the doctor and a thousand for our travel expenses. We were left with just a thousand for our medicines and food for nine days. As we had no money, I left for Chennai on the seventh day after surgery, just after the stitches were removed. I bled continuously for the next two days. I had to wait on the railway platform for four hours to catch the train to Mumbai. We had to lie down, as we were unable to sit after the surgery. People looked at us with curiosity and many made fun of us.

When we went to the women's toilet to urinate, the policewoman shouted at us. 'We know that you have come back after the operation. Why don't you please live like normal humans and get married to women? Why can't you live like good men?'

Moneyless, we had boarded the general compartment without tickets. It was terribly overcrowded and we had to travel sitting for 24 hours. I bled all the way and many of my stitches had come off by the time I reached Mumbai.

My guru took me to a doctor to redo the stitches. She and the other members of my household took me to the doctor every day and looked after me with great love and affection for the next 40 days. They performed various rituals to goddess Pothiraja mata (the presiding deity of the hijra community) that completed my initiation into the hijra community.

**

I was very happy after my nirvanam because I felt I had become a complete woman. I continued with begging and household work but did not get paid for my labour. I did not have the space to demand my share of the earnings. The hijras said that I would have to become more like a woman before they gave me money and sent me to my village. I could not live separately as the hijra community does not permit that.

I wanted to marry a man and live like a family woman. But who would marry a hijra? So I decided at least I must have sex with men. But the rule in our house was that we were not allowed to even see or speak with men. So I left my house and joined another gharana where sex work was permitted. I was now chela to another guru.

I began to seek sex work. But it was not to make money. I got into sex work because I desired men. I was able to have sexual relations with men but it was not satisfying. With clients, you have to do what they want, especially if you need to get paid. I was forced to have sex even when I didn't feel like it because I needed the money. But sadly, I never got to keep even a little money for myself. My guru took the money from my clients on my behalf. I was terrified of asking my clients for money because I feared that they would tell my guru. Sometimes, satisfied clients would pay me ₹5 or ₹10 on their own. Even that money I would give my guru. In spite of taking all the money, my guru never bought me good clothes. She spent the money on going out to bars with her boyfriend.

One day at around 11 am, a local gangster raped me anally at gunpoint. I held onto his legs and pleaded when he wanted me to do things I did not like. He spat abuse at me and forced me to have anal sex. When I screamed in pain, he shut my mouth, whipped out his knife and threatened to slit my throat. I was hurting all over but had to give in to his nasty demands. The skin in my anal region felt abraded and I was bleeding uncontrollably.

When I shouted for help, my guru responded by saying that I would have to satisfy him, as he was a powerful man in the locality. Sex work was possible in our locality only if we did what the goondas ordered us to do. I barely survived the ordeal.

My guru took me to a doctor in Dharavi, who she said was used to treating hijras who had been hurt in these situations. The doctor did not even bother to examine me but simply wrote out a prescription. Back at the jhopdi (urban shanty), I heated water in a broad vessel and poured Dettol into it. I sat across the vessel in such a way that my anal region was immersed in the hot water. It was soothing and temporarily at least relieved my pain. But as soon as the water became less hot, the pain would start all over again. I took the tablets I'd been prescribed and in this way took care of my battered body and anguished soul during this terrible phase of my life.

Later the same goonda was back again. He claimed that while he was having sex, someone had stolen his wristwatch and ₹800 and if they weren't returned to him by evening, he would burn our thatched hut, slash my face and kill all of us.

Terrified, I left for the house of my previous guru. I was put in the house of another hijra, in another part of Mumbai, where everyone did sex work. I worked for two years in that house. The head of that house and my guru shared all the money paid by clients equally. The only income I had was some small money that some clients gave me. Some of the other hijras, who had been in the community for five to six years, wore good clothes and jewellery. Some were accepted by their families and treated well by their gurus. I felt bad that my family did not accept me and that my guru robbed me of all my earnings. So I began to drink excessively.

The head of the house beat me because of my drinking. She was angry that I was wasting my time like this while clients were waiting for me and going away. When I answered back, she hit out at me. While doing so, her glass bangles broke and cut me, I still carry the scar from that wound on my forehead.

Fed up, I decided to return to my birth family in Namakkal. The violence in sex work was impossible for me to put up with any longer. I begged my guru to let me return to my parents. I was certain they would accept me. Reluctantly, they agreed to let me visit them for ten days.

***

I entered Namakkal town dressed in a sari. No one seemed to recognize me. But when I went home, it was as if an earthquake shook my home. When my mother saw me, she wailed, 'I thought you were dead! I wish it had been so! What are these clothes you are wearing? We feared this would happen and so shaved your head. And then you ran away. And now this....'

When he heard my mother's cries, my brother stepped out of the house. 'You motherfucking pottai! Not content with casting our family honour to the winds, you are now dressed in a sari! What guts!' He came towards me with a stick.

'Look! I've been operated upon and I am a woman now! I can now live as I wish. You have no right to beat me any longer. If you do, I'll go to the police!'

Undeterred, he raised his stick. 'Think you are a woman?'

I lifted my sari and showed him, 'Tell me, am I a woman or a man?

My mother covered her face with her hands and wailed.

'He's cut it all off. How could he have done this and still be alive? When he was young, I used to fondle and kiss his bud. He's now standing in front of me like a barren tree!'

Soon the neighbours gathered around me and questioned my decision and ordered me to give up my costume and disguise.

'I didn't change my gender because I was crazy! I feel like a woman. I want to stay true to my feelings and so I've changed into a woman. And I am going to live as one.' I said this with finality.

Surprisingly, it was my father who took it stoically and put an end to all the speculation. Although he was extremely sad at what I had done, he said, 'Look, we did our best. We beat him, shaved his head. Who can change what has been ordained. Let him be and give him some food.'

I stayed at home for a while. But I was completely dependent on my family for every little thing. With hardly any education, what job could I get? I could no longer work with my brothers in the lorry business because I now looked like a woman. And they were constantly scolding and beating me. Even my mother taunted me.

She said, 'Look at what you have become. You have no money and who will feed you for free in this house?'

***

Fed up, I decided to go back to Mumbai to my hijra community. This time I informed my family and went to Bengaluru where I joined a hijra group. I became a sex worker in my new guru's hamam. I lived with her and ten other hijras in the house. I told her that I would not share my earnings with her. She asked me to pay a fixed amount every day for food and shelter. For five years, I did sex work in the streets of Bengaluru. I understood that I would get respect only if I earned. I also saved from my earnings. Whether I went out for sex work or not, I had to give my guru ₹200 every day. Only then could I live in her house.

Occasionally I gave my guru and my family some money. I realized that I was treated with respect within my family and the hijra community only when I did this. I went home every now and then and gave my father the money I had earned. I told him that I had begun dancing and the money came from this. I kept quiet about sex work. The visits home would sometimes last ten days. By then, they let me move about freely and did not restrict me in any way. My family accepted me when I gave them gifts and money. When I didn't, my brothers made fun of me.

When I travelled by bus, women would not sit next to me if they knew I was a hijra. People in the bus teased me all the time. Some men would try to grope me or try funny business with their feet.

My life as a sex worker was very difficult and scary. I ventured out of the hamams onto the streets of Bengaluru for sex work. I pretended to be a woman while seeking clients. Nobody would come to me if they knew I was a hijra. People in cars would pick me up. Most people think that sex work is fun and done only by people who are bored or want to have some 'fun'. But in reality, street based sex work is dangerous. We have to duck behind a bush or seek some little privacy wherever we can find it and finish the job as quickly as possible.

Will someone see us? What if we are caught? We never know when we are likely to be rounded up by the police for 'criminal' behaviour or harassed by rowdies and pimps. And there are clients who will not hesitate to kill us. Many of them often refuse to pay. And if we demand money, they threaten to kill us.

I regularly faced police harassment. Several times, the other hijras and I were chased by policemen who followed us in plain clothes. They slapped me and chased me away before I could get money from my clients. They also took money from me. Even before I made my boni (first earning for the day), they would march me to the police station. I gave them money because I was frightened of them.

I have been dragged into police vans while walking in the streets. At the station they beat, kicked and humiliated me with questions like, 'How come you have a woman's body? Show us!' They would keep me there for two days and torture me. No case was ever registered. They would then drag me to court. At the entrance, they would make me give them money. Say ₹200, and then tell me to get lost.

One day when I was looking for clients, some policemen stopped me and forced me to trap people for them. They lay in wait and collared the clients who approached me to discuss my rate. A few people who stopped to ask for directions also got arrested. They caught ten people this way and then beat me up and warned me not to be seen again or they would shut me up in jail for the next six months.

In another incident, the police arrested me and illegally detained me for two days at the Cubbon Park Police Station. They tortured me physically and verbally abused me. I was forced to eat off the floor and then wash and clean the floor. During such incidents, I wept bitterly. I wondered why I was suffering like this and whether all this was because I was into sex work. If other job opportunities were available, I could live like other women. I wept because I knew that other options did not exist for me.

***

I decided not to do sex work any more. How long could anybody deal with all these things? I wanted to live like other women and so returned to Namakkal. I tried to get a job in telephone booths, cloth stores and provision stores. But no one was ready to employ me because I was a hijra. I could not even think of getting a government job as my school certificates declared that I was male.

I bought a two-wheeler and registered the vehicle as a man, in my male name, as there was no provision to change my name in official documents. I learnt driving but the authorities refused to grant me a license, they said they had 'never had a case like this before'. I got angry and threatened to expose them to the media. Finally they gave the license but prefixed my name Revathi to my male name.

My strongest desire was to marry the man I liked and find a suitable job. But ironically, in trying to become a woman I had ended up living the life of a hijra among other hijras. Having no option for survival, I was forced to take up sex work. I had to buy the love of those around me, including my family, with money. I had to deal with the harassment of police and goondas. The legal system refuses to provide people like me with facilities or assistance. Suffering all this, I wanted to end my life.

When she saw how depressed I was, my mother said, 'This is why we beat you because we did not want you to become a hijra. What is the use of being depressed now? Are you now unhappy in this woman's disguise?'

I told her, 'It's not what you think. I want to live the life of a woman. I am what I want to be. I am unhappy because I can't find a decent job or get married.'

My mother was shocked that I had dreams about getting married to a man.

'Will you be able to bear a child for him? You being a hijra is enough humiliation for us. If you get married, the little dignity we have left, will also go.'

Even if my dreams had to be bundled up in a gunny bag and forgotten, I felt that others like me should not end up the way I had done. What could I do to ensure that? And how? I didn't know. It was at this point that I came in contact with Sangama, a Bengaluru-based organization that works for the rights of gender and sexual minorities. This was a turning point in my life in more ways than one.

2

Finding My Daughters

I often find it strange that a string of seemingly random events and people will come into your life and that will enable you to pursue some of your dreams. My strongest desire was to live as a woman. Another thing I wanted badly was to give up sex work completely. Today, when I look back, I can say that making your desires come true depends entirely on the strength of your convictions and the availability of opportunities. And it is also equally true that if your desires are strong, you will seek out the opportunities until you find them.

I am reminded of an incident in Namakkal. Once I was riding my scooter through the crowded streets of the town. I stopped near a group of auto rickshaw drivers and heard them speculating about whether I was a man or woman. Most of them felt I was too tall and heavily built for a woman. A few said I had cut my hair too short and it looked masculine! I was enraged when I overheard these nasty remarks. I felt that they had no business to talk in such a demeaning manner about me.

I walked up to them and shouted at them. 'So you want to know whether I am male or female? Should I tell you or should I show you that I am not a man but a woman? Looks like this is what you do for a living!'

They were clearly not used to being confronted like this. They immediately defused the situation and said that they were not talking about me. I refused to believe them. I felt that they had to be taught a lesson or this would keep happening repeatedly.

I stood in the middle of the road and yelled, 'Dai! So do you want to lay bets on who's fat, who's thin, who's a man or woman? What do you fellows get out of talking like this? Listen, I am a pottai! I was a man who changed into a woman. If you had one like me in your family, would you place bets on a person like me?'

By now the drivers had begun to slink away. A huge crowd of men and women gathered. Many of them were supportive of me. They felt that men who teased women in public needed to be taught a lesson.

I felt so happy that a few people understood my feelings. It was such a pleasant surprise to know that they did not hate or fear me but were genuine in their sympathy for me. I realized that I was merely going through all that a woman always goes through in public. Maybe a bit more. But I was happy that I had the guts to yell back at my tormentors and confront them. How many women are able to that?

There is this powerful urge within me to take on the wrongs in society. I just can't look the other way when I see some injustice. I wonder if it is because I was born a male and then turned into female that gives me the courage to be confrontational in public places. I wonder if I could have done what I did in this situation, if I had been born female.

Some days after this incident I decided to return to Bengaluru. There were several reasons for my decision. My brothers were ashamed to be seen with me. Several people seemed hesitant to talk with me in public places. In such an atmosphere of avoidance and suspicion, is it any wonder that people like me seek out others like myself?

So I returned to Bengaluru and went back to the Ulsoor hamam where I had lived earlier. It was back again to sex work. There was no other way for me to earn a living. One day when I was sitting on the steps at the entrance to the hamam, three people came to meet me.

They came up to me and said, 'Mummy! Paampaduthi!'

As soon as I heard the word 'Mummy', I knew that they were English-speaking and educated.

'Come, ma! Where are you from?'

From what they told me, it seemed that they were from Bengaluru, although each lived in a different part of the city. I noticed that they spoke to each other in fluent English.

'Mummy! We are friends! We've seen you on this road many times and we've always wanted to talk with you. But we were scared to approach you. But today we decided that somehow we must talk to you. You are very beautiful. We feel like just admiring you all the time.'

'Tell me, you've applied kohl to your eyes. What if someone you know sees you? What if they go and tell your families?'

'That's what we are always afraid of! So we seek out parks, bathrooms, apply kohl and wear pottu (bindi or geometric designs worn by Hindu women on their foreheads). And we go to places where no one knows us. On our way home, we rub all this off. But we don't want to lead this sort of double life; play this game of constant hide and seek. Right now we are neither here nor there. We want to live like you; have the operation done and live like a woman. Mummy, will you accept us?'

Their words reminded me of my own extremely painful decision to live like a woman. And how it was nearly impossible for me to do so with dignity and respect. I recalled having to run away from my home to Delhi and then Mumbai, and now Bengaluru. But now I was living like a fugitive; hounded by the law and police and harassed by goondas and pimps. I did not want these young people to go through the same pain and anguish.

'Well, like you, I too wanted to become a woman. All I can tell you is that this is an extremely difficult life and you will have to cope with a lot. I still do every day. My advice to you young people is that you must live with your families, complete your studies and find a decent job.'

But I reassured them that I understood their feelings; I empathized with their desire to live as women.

'You can spend time with us, sing, dance and have fun! But I don't know if you should get the operation done, give up your studies and suffer like us. Do you know how difficult this life is? If you want to, why don't you stay with us, wear saris, and after you've experienced all of that, go back to your homes in men's clothes? If you become like us, then life is not going to be easy,' I tried to reason with them.

The three young ones were not prepared to take my advice.

'Mummy! We are sure people said the same thing to you when you were like us. Our feelings and desires are not different from what you experienced back then. Even if you advise us against it, we want to have the operation. Please tell us where to get it done.'

I was certain that I did not want them to go through all the pain and humiliation I faced on a daily basis. I did not want to lure them instantly with false promises. I did not say, 'Vaa di! Come, I'll get you operated, if you want it so badly!'

So I refused to give them the information. Instead, I sent them off with some more well meaning advice. I fervently hoped they would listen to me.

But the youngsters were not prepared to listen. Instead, they sought the help of another hijra who accompanied them to Dindugul (where I too had undergone the operation). All three of them underwent castration there. When they came to see me two weeks later, I was shocked to see them.

'Amma, mata....'

As soon I saw them, I knew that they had been operated. How was I so sure? There is a wise saying in Tamil, *oru paambin kaal paambinaal taan ariyum,* only a snake can discern the legs of another snake. The peculiar way they walked with their legs apart, their hesitant faces, downcast eyes, the tiredness and the yearning on their faces, was enough for me. After all, I had been in the same place not so long ago.

I was angry with them when I saw that they had not heeded my well-meaning advice. Even then I knew that they would not listen to me. But I was frank with them because I wanted them to know about the realities of life after the operation. To live as a trans woman is not easy at all because our society still does not accept trans women as 'real' women.

However, today as an activist I know what drives young people to undergo surgical sex change to transform into a woman. Society boxes people into two watertight compartments—male/female or girl/boy. If you are male, you must have a penis. A female must have vagina and breasts. People like us, who are born male, have feminine feelings. But we feel trapped in male bodies. Because people reflect societal values, we feel that the only way we can satisfy our overwhelming desire to be considered women is by surgically removing our male organ. We hate even looking at it and hence we want to chop it off. Maybe if the gender perspectives and perceptions of the mainstream were more flexible and accommodating of difference, we would be able to find other ways of 'finding' ourselves.

Although I was angry, seeing them so forlorn and desperate, I empathized with them. After all, I too hadn't listened to my guru who wanted me to wait for some more time before I underwent castration. I realized that there was no point asking them why they had disobeyed me. There were far more serious aspects that had to be immediately looked into. Based on my experience, the castration or surgical sex change is just one part of our journey towards womanhood. Nobody prepares us for life after this all-important physical change.

If there is an accident you witness on a road, you have two options. You can either not be bothered (which is how most people behave) or you can decide to offer help. I realized that what the three young trans women needed was not long lectures about obedience, but unconditional support and counselling. After all, don't I know the pain of having changed my sex and the difficulty of life after that? And so, unconditional support was what I decided to offer them.

'I can see that you've had the operation. In whose house are you living now that you've had it done?'

One of them, known as Famila, spoke first.

'I stole money from my parents, pawned some of the family jewellery and the land title deed of the house to raise money for the three of us to undergo the operation. We gave all the money to the hijra who took us to Dindugul. But now she wants more money from us and says that what we gave her barely covered the cost of the operation. As we did not have the money, she refused to let us stay with her. We've come to you, please do not send us away!'

There was something powerful and yet vulnerable about the way Famila spoke. I simply could not ignore her request. But at the same time such a move was completely against the norms and social customs of the hijra community. To complicate matters, Famila's parents had filed a police case against the hijra community on the charge that they had forcibly castrated their son.

My gurubais or hijra elders opposed the move vehemently. They were firm that a person wishing to undergo sex change must first join the hijra community and then undergo castration only after a two-year period. They warned me against taking these three obstinate young hijras as chelas.

'Look, they are from the city and also educated. If you accept them as your chelas, their families will blame you for what has happened. Also, they are not like us. They did not want to live with us, learn about our culture and way of life. They went off on their own and got themselves operated. If you are a pottai, you have to know all that there is to know about a pottai's life. You have to respect your gurus, nanis and earn for them and look after them. And only when a guru allows it, a chela gets operated. These three have disrespected all of us and have had themselves operated on their own.'

I was in a dilemma. I asked the trio again, 'Why did you do this even after I persuaded you not to get operated? And you do exactly that and now come and fall at my feet!'

They were in tears. 'Amma! Please accept us as your daughters and teach us right from wrong. If you don't accept us, we have no choice but to die! If our families come and ask for us, we will tell them that we got operated because it was a personal choice for each of us.'

It was the most difficult decision I had to make. On the one hand, I felt their pain and despair and wanted to give them a place where they would be safe; a sanctuary that would be a refuge for them. On the other hand, I knew that they had violated community norms and I too had to abide by the rules of my community. Finally, however, my empathy for them prevailed. Although it was considered taboo in the hijra community, I accepted them as my daughters. They were known as Famila, Ritu and Mayuri. Although all three of them were male bodied when they first came to me, Ritu and Mayuri looked feminine. Famila, on the other hand, was tall, slim and beautiful.

I knew I couldn't have biological children. But I could give my love and affection to these three girls. After all, isn't motherhood all about being nurturing and caring? Although this is the basic sense in which the hijra culture was made, to provide mutual love and care, there are a few hijras who see chelas as just investments; who will earn and bring money back for them. It's like politicians spending money for elections, in the hope that they can recover and more than make up for what they have spent themselves! But for me, the blessing of saying that these girls are my daughters was far more meaningful than other mundane considerations. Love simply cannot be equated with money. As in any other society, there are tales of exploitation as well as incredible support amongst hijras also.

Since they were friends, all three wanted to become my chelas. Sensing that my gurubais would resent this, I told them that I could accept one of them as my chela and the other two would be chelas of my gurubais. But the trio was firm and insisted that all of them wished to be my chelas. Surprisingly, my gurubais gave in.

I gave them a place to stay in the hamam and decided to wait for the customary period of 40 days before I took them to my Nayak's house in Hyderabad in order to accept them as chelas in her presence. But all three of them left the hamam before the stipulated period. Mayuri, the oldest, healed first, while she was in the hamam with me. She then decided to go back to her family in male attire, as if she had not had the operation. Famila called up her parents and informed them about the operation and then went home in male clothes. Ritu went away with her lover.

All three of them behaved contrary to hijra norms after nirvana which said that one should not look at a man in the face until the 40-day period is over and the rites have been done. The trio left because they told me that their families were searching for them and they did not want to land me in trouble. But they promised to return in time for the ceremony. My gurubais spoke to me about the rituals to be done for my three chelas,

'All of us pottais have been obedient to our gurus. We did not mind the beatings and verbal abuse we got from them. We served them, earned for them and looked after them. Only then did we go for nirvaanam. And now, look at these three, they spent their own money and got nirvaanam done. And now you have to spend money and take them to Hyderabad! What if they run away after the rituals? What is the guarantee that they will earn for you?'

I thought very differently. 'If they have truly accepted me as their mother, they won't leave me. I don't intend to do the rituals with the expectation that they will pay me back in some way or the other. I'll do them as a mother would do for her daughters.'

My gurubais were furious with me. 'You mad woman! Why did you think your guru paid for your nirvaanam? Because she saw you as a cash cow that she can milk dry! Remember, you earned the right to have your operation by your behaviour and respect for your guru! Isn't that the custom among us?'

I decided to speak my mind and put an end to this argument. 'Look! These pottais have gone and done the operation. They want to be my daughters and are literally begging and crying that I accept them. I can't talk now about a chela's obligations to a guru. I have to fulfil a guru's responsibility and I wish to do it wholeheartedly. It's fine if they decide to stay with me. But it's also fine with me if they live elsewhere. I am happy I have these daughters.'

I bought all that was required for the pothiraja mata pooja that was the main ritual. I bought all the things they would need—saris, nose rings and anklets. They arrived a day before the ceremony. As I could not afford to hire a hall, I performed the function in the hamam itself. My gurus and gurubais were present. I later took the three girls to Hyderabad, adopted them and did whatever was expected to be done according to tradition.

Ritu and Mayuri left the hamam, as they were unable to fit into the hamam culture of cooperative living. Famila stayed with me for some time. However, she too found the restrictions in the hamam too stifling. Famila was a free bird. She lived life on her own terms. She wore shorts, jeans, T-shirts, smoked and read an English newspaper every day. She often crossed her legs when she sat.

My gurubais were not amused. Not in the least.

'Look at your chela! Just because she speaks English, does she think she is special? As women we are expected to get up early, cook, clean and take care of the home and the family. But look at this pudungi (sassy girl)! The haughty girl gets up late and opens her eyes only if there is tea and the English newspaper! Who does she think she is? Some maharani? And on top of everything, she smokes like a man!'

Finally Famila realized that she was a misfit amongst the hijras in the hamam. So she decided to rent an independent house and live by herself. My three daughters invited their parents to discuss their new lives with them. Famila's parents asked her to return home, but insisted that she wear male clothes. When she refused, her father cut off relations with her. Her mother and brother, however, continued to visit her. I continued to live in the hamam. I wished them well and felt secure that wherever they were, they would always be my daughters. I was certain that I did not want to impose myself on my chelas just because I was their guru. I did not wish to curb their freedom in any way. It was enough for me that they lived happily somewhere. If they needed me for support, I was always there for them.

All this was considered radical in the hijra community in the 1990s. Today as an activist, I am able to see things in perspective. Even today, the hijra community is hierarchical and traditional in its organization. And even back then, I was opposing this with my insistence on treating my chelas as equals and refusing to exercise my power and control over them. Just because I abided by the tenets of the hijra community in Mumbai, Delhi and now in Bengaluru, how could I expect my chelas to follow that too? After all, they were the next generation and had their own dreams and aspirations for a better life. If they wished to live like modern girls, who was I to prevent them from doing so?

My chelas chose to live independently. They did sex work. They had lovers. By doing so, they showed the world that they could live independently as women. Whenever I visited them I felt afraid. What if the neighbours came to know I was a hijra? Even my chelas had this fear. Because in the neighbourhood they passed themselves off as women when they rented houses and described their partners as their 'husbands'. It was different in the hamam because the whole world knew that all of us were hijras. Personally, I was comfortable with the hamam culture but I did not impose it on my chelas.

My chelas were city bred educated girls born and brought up in Bengaluru. They spoke English fluently, dressed in Western clothes and went to bars and discos. All this was unheard of in the hijra culture where we wore only saris and salwar kameez.

Whenever I saw them dressed this way, I also wanted to dress like them. They always addressed me as 'Mummy' and when all of us went out together, I really felt I was indeed their mother. My three chelas gave me an opportunity to nurture them and love them unconditionally—like a mother. The relationship with my chelas enabled me to experience the joys of motherhood despite not being their biological parent. Our relationship has always been a source of deep satisfaction for me.

3

A Turning Point

One day, sometime in 1999, Famila said to me, 'Mummy! There's an organization called Sangama meant for people like us. They have completed one year and are hosting a party. Let's go!'

Famila and my two other chelas were aware of Sangama even before their operation. I was skeptical and hesitant to go. I had no belief in such things. Who will work for people like us? But since Famila insisted, I went just to please her.

When I entered the Sangama office, I was in for several surprises. The people at the centre received us with warmth and affection. Most people expressed their love and affection by hugging even those whom they did not know. What struck me most was that all of them spoke such fluent English. I felt shy to speak to them, as I did not know English. But I was awestruck when I saw my chelas speak to them fluently in English and shake hands with them. Until then, the jamaat was my world; my universe. I knew of no other existence outside it. Today, when I look back I can confidently say that that moment was an eye opener for me.

When I was sure nobody was looking at us or could hear us, I drew Famila aside and whispered, 'Are they also people like us?'

'No, they are not. They are gay,' replied Famila.

'Gay?' I asked puzzled.

'They are homosexuals.'

Famila then introduced me to some of them who greeted me with a breezy, 'Hi'. I responded with the Tamil greeting, 'Vanakkam'.

This was when I came to know of the existence of elite, urban, English speaking gay men and lesbians. It was also a defining moment in my life because I realized that there was a huge gulf that separates working class, non-English speaking sexual and gender minorities from their affluent and educated counterparts. Later, as an activist, I decided to focus exclusively on the needs and rights of non-English speaking gender and sexual minorities as they are disadvantaged in every possible way.

Famila introduced me to activist Elavarathi Manohar, who started Sangama. He explained to me that Sangama was a documentation centre that collected and filed information from newspapers, magazines and the internet about gays, lesbians and other sexual and gender minorities. Of particular interest to Sangama were the widespread instances of human rights violations and denial of rights of sexual and gender minorities. More importantly, he told me that Sangama provided a free and safe space for people to express their sexual orientation and gender identity without fear of ridicule or punishment. Having coped with so much confusion over my gender identity, all by myself, with no one to turn to for support and strength, I immediately realized what a blessing such a space could be for people like us.

'Do hijras, people like me, come too?' I asked him.

'Famila used to come here when she was in male dress. Now she's brought you. We also collect and document information on hijras—the physical and psychological changes they undergo when they opt for sex change and the violence they experience in their families, school and larger society, especially law enforcing agencies.'

I then explained to him about the difficulties of a hijra way of life—especially for those who undergo sex change surgery and wish to live like women. The only options for us are street based sex work and begging—both highly stigmatized work. We are favourite targets for the police and rowdies and are not accepted by our families.

'I wish to help people like me. Do you think I can find a job here?'

'We are trying to raise funds for such a position in the organization. As soon as we are ready, we will let you know. We need someone as committed and passionate as you to speak on behalf of such people,' he said.

I told him that when they were ready, they could send word through Famila. For several days after the meeting, Sangama was always in my thoughts. If only I got a job here, what couldn't I do to improve the lives of hijras like me?

****

My wish was granted. Three months after I visited Sangama, I got a job offer from them. My job was that of a documentation assistant with a monthly salary of ₹2500.

I decided to join Sangama. However, it was a difficult decision for me for several reasons. The salary was low, much less than what I earned through sex work. Would I be able to manage on this paltry salary in a metro like Bengaluru? Meanwhile, my parents were unhappy with my new job as it meant that I could no longer regularly send them money as I used to earlier.

But for me, it was liberation. Liberation from the demeaning street-based sex work that robbed me of my dignity and subjected me to numerous violations. I have always been disgusted by the notion of women as mere sex objects designed solely for male gratification and the control they exerted over our bodies. I was into sex work only because I had no other options. But I must admit that in my early days of sex work, I did look for sexual gratification. There *were* a few caring, loving male clients and such rare opportunities allowed me to experience heterosexual love that I so desired as a woman. But such beautiful experiences were more of an exception than a rule.

My decision to give up sex work was personal. But even today, I work for the rights of sex workers. Despite years of activism, I find that people are still unable to come to terms with sex work as something that is done by women in desperate situations. These women need to be treated with dignity too.

Money has never been everything to me. I therefore decided to take up the Sangama offer because it would enable to me to live with dignity. I now had a job that gave me an opportunity to work for my community. The pull of social change was difficult to resist. I was hopeful that based on my performance; Sangama would pay me better in the days to come.

No more sex work. When I informed my guru of my momentous decision, she was shocked.

'What sort of work is this that gets you only ₹2500 every month? If you do danda (hijra slang for paid sex) on MG Road or Brigade Road, you will earn more!'

I refused to be cowed down by her. Instead I spoke firmly with my guru.

'Amma! People like us have only done sex work and begging forever. How much longer should we do this? And if we continue to do only this, how will society respect us? The hijras of my generation want to do something different. We want to tell others about our lives so that they can understand us. And we too want to live like those around us.'

Finally my guru relented. She said, 'It's your life. Do what you like.'

***

I joined Sangama as an office assistant in charge of documentation. At that time, in the late 1990s, not much was known about sexual and gender minorities. But there is enough evidence in the history of our country to suggest that hijras are mentioned in Hindu mythology and were also part of the Mughal palaces where they served as handmaidens of the queens.

My job involved filing clippings from newspapers and magazines, and reports pertaining to sexual and gender minorities, particularly the human rights violations they faced and downloading material from the internet. I would cut out the portions marked for filing and stick them on white sheets, categorize them into sections, with relevant details such as the date, name of the publication and the sexual/gender minority that was in focus—queer, gay, lesbian, male to female transgender, female to male transgender and sex worker. But I also did other things as well. For instance, looking after the accounts, the library and even making tea and getting things needed for the office.

Sangama literally opened several doors for me. As a trans woman, I took on a new avatar as Revathi after my transition to a woman through surgery. In Sangama, I took on yet another avatar, as an activist. It was a slow process, and I absorbed all the learning, through several opportunities that I had. I participated in several interesting workshops, seminars and training programmes on the human rights violations of other marginalized communitiess, including dalits and adivasis. I also gained insights into the politics of communal clashes and the impact of wars waged by powerful countries. It was a splendid opportunity to interact with members of different communities and meet people from all walks of life. Today, when I look back, I can proudly say that the outcome of nearly a decade of association with Sangama is that it was there that I took the first steps towards becoming an activist.

Shortly after I joined Sangama, Famila too was appointed as Hijra Outreach Coordinator. One of my earliest experiences as Sangama staff was participating in the Women's Day function organized on March 8 by Mahila Okutta—a federation of NGOs working on gender issues in Karnataka.

The preparation for this grand event began as early as five months before the actual event. We held weekly and biweekly meetings to decide on the theme for the year based on regional realities. I met several women leaders from the dalit, adivasi and child rights movements. I was the only trans woman in the meetings and all of us got to know each other well.

The participants frankly shared with me their reservations and apprehensions about the transgender community.

'We are afraid of them. Even if we sit next to them in a bus, we move away. But when we see you, we don't feel the same way. You look like a woman and no different from us. You don't wear too much make up,' they said.

It is true that some trans women wear a lot of make up because it is necessary for their sex work or simply because they like to do so. I too did that when I was a sex worker before I joined Sangama. Nevertheless their comments made me question several popular stereotypes. I realized that people judge trans people solely by our appearance, which is misleading. For example, some trans women look manly but dress in a sari. While others look feminine but have a manly voice. Why do we believe that if you are a woman you must be small built, have a soft voice, look soft, have breasts, long hair, and dress modestly? Why don't people accept trans women who are big built and use make up?

The Women's Day celebration was the right platform for me to address such misconceptions and stereotypes about what it means to be a woman or a man in today's world. The event began with a massive rally by all women's groups from Karnataka. It concluded with a public meeting, where speakers were given five minutes to address the audience. The theme that year was the unnatural death of women.

I read out the following poem *Conception to Cemetery* that I had specially composed for the occasion.

You died as soon as you knew your face, while you were
still an embryo;
You died after you drank the poisonous datura juice
as a baby
You died after you were robbed of your virginity
as an adolescent
You died after having given dowry in your marriage
You died while cooking in the kitchen
You died in the bedroom as your drunkard husband
forced you to have sex with him
You died dressed in white widow's clothes
You died on the funeral pyre of your husband.

Famila and I led by example. We were in the forefront of those who identified themselves as hijras and asserted their sexual rights. Before I joined Sangama I was scared to even admit that I am a hijra and that I did sex work. I was hesitant to speak to the media about my hijra identity. I was worried about what my family, friends and neighbours would think of me when they knew I did sex work. Was it 'wrong' to be a hijra and do sex work?

However, once I joined Sangama I realized it was not my fault. It certainly was not my fault that my gender did not match with what people thought me to be; it certainly was not my fault that I was thrown out of my family; it certainly was not my fault that I was forced to discontinue schooling. Then why are we subjected to such terrible violations and denied our basic rights as human beings? And under such circumstances what else could people like me do except begging and sex work?

At Sangama, I acquired a lot of insights into several aspects of gender, sex and sexuality. I realized that gays and lesbians don't usually have a different gender identity; but rather, have a sexual orientation that is different; of being attracted to members of the same sex. For instance, when you look at them, they look like any one else, and unless and until they disclose their sexual orientation no one can make anything out.

But when people look at hijras, they immediately sense we are different. All children, whose gender does not match with their sex, are known as gender non-conforming children. I was one too. Children like us face problems even early in life. The way we walk, like to dress and play is just the opposite of gender norms considered appropriate for one's biological sex. For example, even as a child, I loved to play with girls, help my mother at home and dress like a girl. That's because society believes that if one is male, he should behave in a particular way and if one is female, she should behave differently.

Even today, people identify me as a trans woman based on my voice and height. Most male to female transgender people have their names in their birth and school certificates as male. After we have transitioned, people point out the discrepancies between our original names and new names. There is no provision to change the names in the original certificates. How then will we get admission into colleges, get jobs and get passports? In such circumstances, people who undergo sex change are not viewed as people and are thus denied their basic rights.

Transgender people are the most visible among gender minorities. Most people think that we are just lazy and so just get into easy options like begging or sex work. Let me ask you, do you think street based sex work is easy or fun? Do you know how vulnerable we are at the hands of the police, rowdies and clients? When people see us loitering on the roads, they immediately telephone the higher police officials and lodge a complaint about us. Often they even accuse the cops of not doing anything about us. In turn, the higher officials in the police hierarchy pressurize their juniors to arrest us. Often, we are arrested for a variety of false charges. These include accusing us of obscene behaviour and the use of vulgar language in public, false charges of dealing in drugs, pickpocketing, chain snatching and false cases being foisted on us. To escape, we need to bribe them or meekly put up with the harassment.

We have to solicit clients on the road, often from 7 pm to 11 pm by flagging a car or motorbike. The police pounce on us and question us about why we are there at night. If we manage to get a client, we have to have sex, ducking behind a bush, a lodge or in a car. The police always hound us. In such situations, just walking on the road is a crime for hijras.

Some of our clients think that we are biological women. Others specifically seek out trans women. One of our advantages is that we have no fear of unwanted pregnancy. We perform oral, anal and thigh sex. If we earn ₹500 a day, we have to pay off the police, the rowdy (besides giving him free sex!) and the jamaat. We then take home just ₹100.

We face civic problems as well. Few house owners are willing to rent their houses to us. Nobody would let out their houses to us in prime areas of a city. If at all we get houses, it is only in the slums and they charge us almost double! The reasons are many. They believe that we are loud and use the place for sex work. Besides, as the houses are in commercial areas, they feel that our presence is a source of disturbance and a nuisance to the neighbourhood. And worse, our presence would be an incentive for the young men in the neighbourhood to become involved as our clients in sex work.

When we analysed these problems, Famila and I wondered how we were going to address such serious issues. It was very important to address pressing issues such as violence, exclusion, stigma and discrimination experienced by most transgender people. And this was central to the activism that Famila and I spearheaded.

All of us were new to such work. But we were passionate about the cause. We wrote proposals for space and hiring more staff. Finally, we were ready to launch our first initiative—crisis intervention. It was a sphere in which I invested my passion and compassion as an activist.

4

A Struggle for Human Dignity

Sangama's first community outreach initiative was in crisis intervention for the transgender community. During those days Sangama provided twenty-four hour support to the community by actively intervening in any crises community members may have had to face. We formed a four-member crisis intervention team along with full time legal support. Any member of the community could call one of us when faced with trouble—usually harassment from the police or rowdies. The staff was trained to respond appropriately in such situations, especially to negotiate assertively and effectively with law enforcing agencies.

For instance, we were given intensive training in how to talk to the police and how to present our case assertively and convincingly. We also acquired considerable legal literacy in aspects such as FIRs (First Information Reports) and the fact that an FIR needed to be filed before a person could be arrested. We also learnt that it was mandatory to give the accused individuals time to inform their families, friends or an organization, and ensure that the accused were not subjected to violation and instead produced before court according to legal protocols. We learnt that if arrested, trans women had to be lodged in female cells and not in male cells as was routinely done. Each of these aspects was new to us. Until then, we had just accepted violence from the police and goondas and tried to negotiate in our own ways. Now, we learnt the legal way.

The training was an eye opener for me for several reasons. As a trans woman, I was no stranger to brutal harassment at the hands of the police and rowdies. The police perceive transgender individuals as public nuisances and as a source of shame and hence drive us away from the city limits. It is common for them to foist false charges on transgender people, accusing us of chain snatching, stripping in public and pick pocketing.

I don't say that some members of the transgender community don't indulge in such activities. They do. But isn't it wrong to brand all of us as criminals? After all, don't members of the cisgender community (so called 'normal' people) also indulge in such illegal activities? But then do we brand all men and women as criminals? Such branding of entire communities is always reserved for minorities.

As part of the crisis intervention team, we were against such sweeping generalizations of criminality of a particular community. When negotiating with the police, we told them that we represent a human rights organization. We insisted that when transgender individuals were arrested at night they must be lodged in a remand home and not in the police station.

However, what I did not anticipate was the numerous challenges that I would face in sensitizing not only the police but also the transgender community, in other words, our own community. I was in charge of the trans women intervention services. I undertook field visits on a daily basis to interact with the community and talk to them about Sangama and the services it offered.

Initially the transgender community was hostile and resistant to the very idea of crisis intervention. For most of them, their immediate goal, when arrested, was to free themselves from the clutches of the police. They had neither the inclination nor the motivation to cooperate in the judicial enquiry process. They argued with me. 'Why go to court? Your NGO will come today and be gone tomorrow. But we have to face these people (police) on a daily basis. Tomorrow, we have to go on the same road to either beg or do sex work. So we want to compromise with the police.'

I realized that the community would not change overnight. And so began a slow long and difficult process of working with them. I patiently explained about Sangama and why it wanted to work for the welfare of the transgender community. I also explained that Sangama was unable to support the entire community as it only had limited funding to support staff salaries. However, the community was still resistant to the idea.

'You are lucky to get a monthly salary and a safe space to work. But what about us? Why do you want us to come to the office? What will you give us in return? Will you give us food, clothes and money?' they retorted.

I knew I had to be tactful and patient. After all, their concerns were genuine and I too had gone through all that.

'We have helpline numbers where they can call us and tell us about the incident, and we then co-ordinate with the other members from the organization to go and resolve the situation. When there is a legal issue, we have our advocates who look into the issue,' I explained to them. Besides, I reiterated to them that unless we, as transgender people, stand up for our rights and challenge false cases, this situation of routine violation will continue.

We were constantly exploited not only by the police, pimps and rowdies, but also by the media and general public. Many writers and journalists have interacted with us, written about us and sold our stories abroad for huge sums of money. Naturally, the community is suspicious even of well meaning intentions. But despite their initial reservations, they slowly began to trickle into the Sangama office. In time, Sangama began to mobilize and collectivize members of the transgender community. It resulted in a community based organization, Vividha, to handle crises in the community.

Vividha was a community based organization of gender and sexual minorities. Around 50-60 people met every Sunday in the apartment where the Sangama office was located. The organization provided members with a safe space for sharing experiences and talking about issues important to them. However, the owner of the apartment became suspicious of us and informed the police. Because we are highly visible as trans people we are criminalized for just being different and become easy targets. We were forced to vacate the office space and relocate.

We highlighted the human rights violations Vividha members were subjected to. We even sent petitions to Sonia Gandhi and we received a communiqué from New Delhi that this was a serious violation of human rights and we should be allowed to continue with our work.

In 2002, Vividha organized a Hijra Habba festival, jointly supported by Sangama and YMCA, Bengaluru. The festival had beauty contests, music and dance. It was a platform for the transgender community to celebrate ourselves. Well known actor and activist Nandita Das and the Police Commissioner of Bengaluru, P.C. Sangliana, were the chief guests. I felt honoured when Nandita Das released my poetry collection. I liked her because of her commitment to social causes and support for marginalized communities. We did not give prizes for the contestants, as we believed that every one of us is inherently beautiful.

The commissioner, however, ruffled feathers by targeting the transgender community. 'Why are you creating public nuisance by chain snatching, indecent behaviour and pick pocketing? We will arrest you,' he said.

Bristling with anger, I confronted him openly.

'Why shouldn't we walk on the roads? We are often arrested for no fault of ours. Where's the proof of our crimes? Even if we do something that is an offence, arrest us legally and prove the charges. Why do the police violate us? Strip us of our dignity? In this world, don't other men and women commit crimes? But then you don't brand all of them, do you? Then why do you do this to us?'

The media highlighted the range of human rights violations experienced by my community, which they felt I had brought out eloquently. But the commissioner stuck to his prejudiced stance.

In 2003, Vividha single handedly conducted the Hijra Habba on a grand scale. My chela and colleague Famila played a major role in organizing this grand show. Articulate and well informed, she highlighted the violations experienced by the community with sensitivity and insight. The Hijra Habba simply affirmed the principle that transgender persons are lawful citizens of our country and our fundamental rights (including civil, political, social, economic and cultural rights) need to be protected and guaranteed through the law and by meaningful engagement by the government and general public.

A turning point for Vividha was its role in crisis intervention in the lives of one of its members. A trans woman and her husband were accosted and beaten up by the police while standing on a road. Our society finds it hard to accept that a trans woman can have a husband. The police thrashed the partner mercilessly.

'She is a trans woman. If you are her husband, what sort of a person are you? Are you man enough? Or are you a hijra too?' they yelled.

Society thinks that vaginal or penetrative sex is the only kind of sex that is 'natural'. Transgender persons are not even regarded as people. We are seen as sexual deviants who are meant to satisfy only the perverse pleasures of male clients. We are not seen as women worthy of love or care. In this instance, a false case was foisted on the woman and her partner was charged as a pimp using her for commercial sex. The police did not value their relationship as legitimate.

The transgender community and Sangama fought the case. We established that the police had slapped false charges and also challenged this in court—the case dragged on for more than a year and finally the police stance was proved false.

Another momentous crisis intervention undertaken by Vividha was what came to be known in activist circles in Bengaluru as the 'Kokila crisis'. Kokila, a 21-year-old transgender woman from Tamil Nadu, lived in Bengaluru where she was a sex worker. On June 22, 2004, Kokila was standing near the NGEF Layout in Bengaluru, when ten men forcibly took her to a plot adjoining the road, where she was gang raped. At some point a couple of policemen arrived on the scene and nabbed two of the culprits, while the rest escaped.

For Kokila, however, the worst was yet to come. How does one respond when protectors of the law turn out to be perpetrators of gruesome violence? Kokila was taken into a room in the Bypanahalli Police Station, stripped naked and bound to a window with handcuffs. The six policemen hit her with batons, abused and tortured her sexually. She was burnt with cigarette butts and burning coir. Later, the policemen took her to a nearby public bathroom and forced her to dress in male clothes threatening to tonsure her head if she did not comply. Then, they took her to the house of another hijra activist Chandini, and searched the house. When Chandini objected, they also abused and threatened her.

All of us strongly condemned the behaviour of the police and lodged a complaint against their atrocities. We were certain that such incidents were not stray occurrences but were part of the ongoing police violence against hijras. We also could see that the level of violence had increased after hijras started protesting against police brutality.

Undeterred, we organized a massive rally of sexual and gender minority individuals to protest against police brutality and pressed for immediate action against the concerned police officials. More than 25 NGOs and human rights activists from Tamil Nadu, Andhra Pradesh, Kerala, Karnataka, Delhi and Mumbai participated in the rally. Fortunately for us, the media was extremely supportive of our cause and exposed the brutal excesses of law enforcing agencies. This success demonstrated the power of collectivization and solidarity in advocacy initiatives. The transgender community, for the first time, saw the power of uniting for a cause and asserting their rights to a life of dignity. 'Hijra rights are also human rights,' was not mere sloganeering but a principle we were keen to see in action.

The massive solidarity against police harassment that was evoked by Kokila's false arrest highlighted how oppressive the state was towards vulnerable minorities like us hijras.

About four years later, in 2008, police from the Girinagar police station in Bengaluru arrested and lathi-charged five hijras for begging, and falsely accused them of extortion. Besides, the Assistant Commissioner of Police and the inspector at the nearby Banashankari Police Station detained several staff members from the crisis response team of Sangama as well as 31 protestors who were demonstrating against the issue. The police threw away the staff ID cards and instead arrested the people who had gone to intervene in the matter. Can't we, transgender people, work in organizations, can't we question atrocities, can't we talk legalities? When police do not follow procedures and instead brutalize us, we confront them and question their actions. The police mock us, 'Oh! So, you people also talk of legalities now!'

Not to be outdone, we filed a case against the police. As head of the crisis intervention team, I chalked out a strategic plan to effectively address the issue. I realized that there was no point in simply antagonizing the police. What we needed was to address this issue sensitively. As a first step, we launched a campaign to reach across to police personnel all over the city. We explained to them the nature of our work and sought their cooperation. At the end of our interaction, we presented with them a floral bouquet. As a next step, we printed a set of 50,000 pamphlets about our cause and distributed it to the public. We also launched a Black Solidarity Day, in which people showed their unstinted support for our cause. The police, meanwhile, realized that that they could no longer get away by harassing hijras.

Society has prescribed gender roles for women and men. Gender non-conforming children are subject to multiple violations even in childhood. Who is there to advocate on our behalf? The media is not sensitive. Transgender individuals are the butt of ridicule and jokes in films and on the streets. Harassment is a way of life for us. We are harassed by parents, teachers, peers, and the police. The media and law only highlight our involvement in street based sex work and begging. Why don't you highlight some of our pressing needs and concerns and the multiple violations and oppressions we experience? Perhaps you don't because we are an invisible minority and not a powerful vote bank.

In early November 2008, the Amrutahalli police pressurized house owners in Dasarahalli, a suburb in North Bengaluru, to evict their transgender tenants. It was an area in which transgender people and the larger community were supportive of each other and living amicably. Surprisingly, some leading news channels and national dailies sensationalized these incidents, portraying the transgender community in a bad light. I was shocked at the sudden turnaround of the media, which had been so supportive in the Kokila crisis.

It was obvious that the police and hijras were in opposite camps and that the former wanted to seek revenge on the hijras for what they perceived as our audacity in openly opposing them and demanding our rights. When we launch a crusade for our rights and confront those who inflict violence on us (police, rowdies, parents and partners) despite our legitimate demands, they manipulate and use loopholes in the law to their advantage. Their attitude seems to be that of vindictive revenge—'If you do this to me, see what I will do! Don't I know the legal aspects that you are aware of?'

The sensational arrest on false charges, subsequent custodial torture and the complicity of the medical establishment in violating a 20-year-old trans woman, Shilpa, is a glaring example of this attitude. Sadly, there are many such instances.

The arrest of Shilpa, a 20-year-old hijra was just the opportunity the police was waiting for. Continuing its vicious campaign against hijras, the Bengaluru police arrested Shilpa, in November 2008 using an old missing complaint from her family. Born as a physiological male, Shilpa, like most hijras, felt that she was a female trapped in male body. Because of attempts by her parents to control her feminine gender expression, she left home, and befriended two hijras, Baby and Mangla, who empathized with her. Although they dissuaded her from running away from home and becoming a hijra, Shilpa was firm in her resolve. She moved in with Mangala and Baby, and later expressed her desire to undergo castration at Cuddapah in early 2008.

During her detention, the police abused Shilpa verbally and physically. Worse, they filed a false complaint against Mangala and Baby for forcibly castrating Shilpa and imprisoned them for two years. Meanwhile, they coerced Shilpa's parents to agree to a penile grafting surgery at a well known corporate hospital in the city, as according to them, Shilpa was a minor when she was castrated. The parents agreed as they were promised a huge sum of money if they cooperated. They then got doctors to reconstruct her penis—a gross violation of her bodily integrity. However, after this procedure was performed, Shilpa's parents did not get the promised reward.

Shilpa had absolutely no desire to undergo penile grafting but was coerced into it. The doctors exploited her for personal fame and a perverse medical experiment. A well known human rights lawyer commented that there are international guidelines and medical protocols to be followed for Sex Reassignment Surgery (SRS), which is a process that is spread over at least three years. In Shilpa's case, it was done almost overnight! So, if we want to undergo SRS legally, there are tedious procedures, but if it is done to us as a violation, then there are a million ways they find to sidestep these. But who will talk about justice for the transgender community?

Shilpa testified in court that she had voluntarily undergone castration when she was 20 years old. It was conclusively proven that the police had foisted false charges on her and the others. Her testimony enabled Mangala and Baby to be released.

Words cannot express what I felt for Mangala, Baby and Shilpa. For no fault of theirs but their decision to be themselves and help each other, they suffered such misery. Mangala and Baby were jailed for two years and eight months. Shilpa does not want the male organ that has been forcefully constructed on her. The surgery itself, apart from the fact that it was non consensual, was of terrible quality. She has been traumatized physically and psychologically to an unimaginable extent. How will the police, the law and the medical establishment redress this? What punishment do they deserve for these horrendous violations?

For people like Shilpa, I and other trans people, where is the law to support us, to validate us, to acknowledge our feelings? Do parents, teachers, friends, doctors, counsellors, have sufficient insight and awareness? For people like Shilpa and I, where is the security and support in childhood? Throughout our childhood and even later, we have been wracked by guilt and shame over why we have feminine feelings in our male bodies. I am certain that female to male trans persons also go through a similar trauma over their masculine feelings trapped in a female body.

Why don't you change your perceptions and negative stereotypes about us? To you, we are still derogatorily to be called ombodhu, ali and pottai, people who kidnap male children, castrate them and push them into begging. If a child doesn't behave, the mother points to us and threatens, 'If you don't behave, I will hand you over to that person who will then take you away to Bombay.' Both law and society criminalize us and treat us as people to be ashamed of. To them, we are untouchables to be avoided at any cost.

5

My Rights as a Trans Woman

Rejected by parents
Rejected by society
Rejected by the world
I sing today.

I am left with neither property
nor pleasure
I am left with neither home
Nor a job.

I was born a man
I have struggled to be as any woman
to be a daughter, a sister
a mother, a grandmother
a grand daughter.

Ours is an excluded
and exiled community
we are the aravanis
the transgender people.

Violated by goondas and the police
criminalized by the law
that fails to understand
our desperation
to live, to exist.

We are called
beggars and sex workers
has this world left us any choice?

We crave for love
we need to love too
as do all human beings.

We will continue to struggle
we ask not for your pity
only your understanding.

We demand acceptance
from parents
from society
from the world
to be human
to live as we have chosen.

Poem originally written in Tamil by Revathi as part of her presentation at the Asia Pacific Court of Women on HIV, Inheritance and Property Rights, Colombo, Sri Lanka

In 2003 an unexpected opportunity came my way. This was an invitation to attend the South Asian Court of Women on Violence and Trafficking in HIV/AIDS to be held in Dhaka. The invitation came through Vimochana, a well known NGO in Bengaluru, which works on gender issues.

I was confused. On one hand, I was excited a the prospect of taking a flight and travelling to a foreign country. It would be my first trip abroad. But I was also worried if I would be able to get a passport.

My fears were certainly valid. Until then, no transgender person had a passport.

The reason it was nearly impossible for people like me to get a valid passport was that as transgender people we had no valid ID proof. At that point, we did not have voter IDs and ration cards. Our only valid document was our school certificate. But here again, was another hurdle. The original name in my school certificate did not match with my current status as a trans woman with a female name. Although after adopting a new name (Revathi), I had gone through the procedural formalities of announcing my name change in two local newspapers, there were no legal procedures for changing it in the original certificates. So the glaring discrepancy persisted and was a major stumbling block.

But I was determined not to give up. Getting a passport was an affirmation of my rights as a citizen of India. There are only two boxes in the passport form: male or female. Of course, this has changed now with the option of TG as a separate column in passport applications but at that time, it was not an option. Another issue is that it is impossible for trans people to provide address proof (as transgender individuals are a migrant community), we did not have any of the required documents or even bank accounts.

However, I decided I would not let any of this stop me. I had with me a letter from Sangama and an affidavit provided by feminist activist Ashwini Sukthankar, as well as my school leaving certificate—this latter as proof of my age. I took these and went to the passport office in Bengaluru. But to my dismay, the first thing the authorities pointed out was the discrepancy in the name in my school leaving certificate (Doraiswamy) and my current name (Revathi).

Although after the sex change operation, I had legally changed my name to Revathi, it did not automatically mean that my gender was now female. There was no legal provision to do that. I told them that I am a trans woman who had undergone a sex change surgery. They insisted that I go to the doctor to get a medical certificate and sent me away.

At the government hospital, I had to face a lot of ridicule and humiliation while I was being medically examined by an obstetrician and a gynaecologist to prove that I was indeed a woman. I put up with all the hardships because I wanted to attend the conference.

At one point I said to the doctors in sheer desperation, 'I don't care if you give me a certificate as male or female. But give me one, please. I need to get a passport to represent my country at an international conference. Am I a terrorist trying to fake a passport? As a doctor, it is your duty to examine me and give me a certificate.'

Finally, I won. I managed to get a medical certificate that I was indeed a female and the passport authorities issued a passport that enabled me to attend the conference. I was the first trans woman in the country to have been issued a passport.

The Courts of Women are public hearings. Held once in four years, the first Court of Women was held in Lahore, Pakistan, in 1992. The term court is used symbolically. In these spaces, the voices of victims and survivors are heard loud and clear, many for the first time. A platform for human rights, the courts highlight with sensitivity and compassion the enormous indignities, oppressions and human rights violations most women experience on a daily basis. But all stories had one common thread—they spoke about the resilience and triumph of the human spirit.

As a trans woman I was asked to speak about the multiple oppressions and violations of human rights that I had experienced and still continue to face on a daily basis. This was the first time a trans woman had been invited to share her experiences. My speech was called 'Violence, dignity and resistance in a transgender world.' My talk traced my childhood, growing up years and finally my experiences as a trans woman that were marked by the stark violence perpetrated by my family, teachers, peers and the state—all because I am differently gendered.

At this point, I must mention that at first the organizers of the conference had requested me to speak about the rehabilitation of transgender people. However, I have no faith in the concept of rehabilitation. Many people tell us that they will give us a sewing machine, cows and goats and teach us how to make Phenyl and pappads. But such piecemeal measures are of no use to transgender people. Instead why don't you give us our rights? What we need is government jobs. For example, a trans woman in a village was given a buffalo. But she did not have the economic means to look after it. When the female buffalo was in estrus, she needed fifty rupees to get the it inseminated. She could get that money only through sex work. What could she do for fodder for the cow? Can she graze the cow in fancy parks? People like us have no homes. Where will we tie the cow? These measures do not work for us.

Rehabilitation, in the true sense of the idea for us, is acknowledging and affirming our human rights. Why do we experience stigma and discrimination? Why do our birth families disown us? Why are we thrown out of our homes and schools? We need policy changes through the government, sensitization for schoolteachers and laws for protecting child rights. All of these are part of long term policy changes towards sustainable rehabilitation for our community. In the absence of all these, the only two options for us are street based sex work and begging.

Society is still negative about transgender people because we are involved in sex work. Like they screw up their noses at dalits and adivasis—and call them 'chee, thu' out of a sense of aversion and disgust, similarly they have the same feelings for trans people across caste. To such people I pose this question: Why can't the government decriminalize sex work? Then, maybe, the stigma would be considerably less.

Personally, however, I have no interest in sex work. It's the biggest violation of bodily integrity when you are coerced into sex when you don't desire it. But society says that only the lazy do sex work! Nothing can be farther from the truth! Street based sex work is risky and dangerous. Only a sex worker knows that. There is no guarantee that you will get back home. One has to face the ever-present danger of harassment by rowdies, pimps, police and clients.

Despite being an activist, as a trans woman, I still experience multiple forms of discrimination in my family, and in public places. Our moralistic and judgmental society wonders why we are like this. But I ask them—can you live like us even for a day? Despite the hurdles, we persist in living the lives we want. Instead of judging us, give us the opportunity to lead a life of dignity and respect just like any other person.

I want to live with my family. Do not discriminate against me on account of my gender. If only people in school had been aware and sympathetic, we would not be in such a situation today! Had they known that gender variation is a spectrum rather than just the given binary of man/woman, perhaps they would have been more accepting of me. What has the government done for differently gendered children at the school and college levels? Has the government ever questioned the parents of such children about why they disown their children?

There are no systems and procedures in place to address our pressing needs and concerns. We need long term solutions; not ad hoc responses. If my parents had allowed me to dress in a sari, why would I have left home? If the government had offered me SRS (Sexual Reassignment Surgery) free of charge, then wouldn't I have taken it? If my school had been accepting of me, would I have quit my studies? Such initiatives must be mainstreamed if we are to be integrated into society.

I highlighted several such concerns of the transgender community at the Dhaka conference. Yet the conference itself was an eye opener for me. Until then, I thought that my story was the worst. But when I listened to several more harrowing stories, my whole perspective on life completely changed. I met several marginalized women such as HIV positive women denied property rights after their husband's death, women trafficked into sex work, survivors of custodial rape, survivors of domestic violence and children being trafficked for camel jockeying. All my bottled up feelings rose to the surface and exploded—feelings that I had pushed deep down within myself and even refused to acknowledge to myself. I formed several meaningful friendships with other women. The three days healed my spirit and gave me renewed strength and energy to take my activism forward.

Four years later, in 2007, I was once again invited to attend the Asia Pacific Court of Women on HIV, Disinheritance and Property Rights, this time in Colombo. I spoke on 'Reclaiming gender spaces', which focused on my struggle to reclaim my share of the family property, which was denied to me on account of my trans woman status.

I was amazed at how much I had grown personally and professionally since the last Court of Women at Dhaka. At that point I was diffident and confused. When I heard that I had to speak at a court, I wondered if it would be like the courts all of us have heard of. As far as we transgender people are concerned, courts of law are mostly non responsive and callous to our needs and concerns. They expect only rigid yes/no responses. But our lives are fluid and there are so many shades of grey. How then do we articulate our needs, concerns and aspirations? At the Dakha conference, something very deep changed within me as I heard the stories of the other participants. It was healing. I felt strengthened and supported because so many people unconditionally stood by us; believed that we too are human beings with every right to a life of dignity. In the intervening period, I grew in ways that I did not think was possible earlier. My activism for the human rights of sexual and gender minorities grew tangibly. I had published my first book; written many poems. I brought all these dimensions to the Colombo Court of Women. I felt I could inspire and mentor others who were in the same position I once was.

While all people struggle at some point in their lives, for transgender people like me, it is a way of life. It was an intense struggle for me to be accepted by my family. When they finally did accept me, I was relieved that I did not have to face this daily tug of war any more. For some time, life seemed to flow smoothly. But soon the ugliness reared it head again; this time, in a way that even I had not anticipated. This was the issue of sharing the family property among my brothers. My three elder brothers argued bitterly with me that since I had become a trans woman, was a member of the hijra community, was single and had no family, I did not need a share in the family property. They ordered me to write a letter to this effect and leave the place.

My father was confused and took me to an advocate. On the way he shared with me his fears that his other sons would deprive me of my rightful share of the family property. When we met the advocate, the latter instructed me to come to court dressed like a man. I disliked his suggestion because I have always felt that my identity was that of a woman. But the advocate explained that the court would refer to me by my former male name and that I could not appear as a woman. He even advised me to cut my hair short and wear trousers and a shirt. Besides, he reasoned, my brothers could always claim that they 'do not know this woman' and that would make it easier for them to usurp my share of the property. Despite all his entreaties and reasoning, I refused.

Disappointed, my father and the advocate discussed the matter between themselves. They then asked me to step inside the room. The advocate asked me whether I trusted my father. I said that I did so absolutely. He then requested me to write a letter authorizing my father to sign on my behalf to get my share and that it could be transferred to my name in due course of time. I also wrote in the letter stating that as I lived away from my native place and being unable to attend the court proceedings due to unavoidable circumstances, I am authorizing my father to sign on my behalf.

I was unaware of the discussions that my father, my brothers and the advocate had regarding the legal proceedings. They asked me to pay ₹40,000 towards the lawyer's fee and the court proceedings. I was aghast, as I had no money with me. I confessed my financial inability to my brothers. They were furious with me and abused me in vulgar language about my life. They then told me that they would give me ₹1 lakh and asked me to give it in writing that I hereafter did not have any claim or connection with the family property and would not interfere in family matters.

As a sex worker I had been supportive of my family. I had even given my father ₹4 lakh to renovate the family home. My father even wrote a will in which he bequeathed the house to me. Fearing that my brothers would deprive me of my inheritance after my father's death, I had even requested my father to register the house in my name.

However, my father said that he would write the will in my sister's name. When I heard this, I felt cheated by my father. Hurt and angry, I demanded that he give back the money I had given him. My father justified his action and said that he was doing so because he feared that I would throw my parents out of the house if it were registered in my name. He even asked for proof that I had given him money. I felt even more hurt by his remark because only I knew the indignities and torture I had undergone to earn that money. Harassed and hounded by the police, pimps, rowdies and clients, I often did not think I would even survive such a dangerously violent life. Every brick in the house knew the tears and toil I had gone through.

Unable to control myself, I stepped out of the house and gave vent to my feelings of having been cheated by my own father. In a desperate measure to end my life, I even poured kerosene on myself. On seeing this, my mother and sister requested my father to register the house in my name. My father also told me that I could not mortgage or sell the house until his death. I agreed to all his conditions and paid ₹30,000 to complete the registration process.

Currently I cannot sell the house or avail any loans against it. Only after the death of both my parents can I do either of these. My family thinks that since I don't have a family of my own, I might misuse the property. Because I am a hijra, they fear that I might give away the house to my community. Of course, for Dalit trans women whose families have no property, the struggle is much harder. However, ugly as it is, personally the struggle has been worth it for me. For I have asserted that hijras too have the right to own property. According to me, it is one small but significant step towards reclaiming our lost spaces.

6

A Writer is Born

Gradually, I began to find my calling as an activist who highlighted the needs, concerns and aspirations of the transgender community. It seemed the most natural thing to happen because I believe that there cannot be a better experience than the one born out of lived reality.

I did not become a trans woman on an impulse or because I was so arrogantly self-centered that I wished to disown every trace of my maleness. Rather, I became a trans woman because I had always felt that I was a woman. But a woman trapped in a male body. I wanted to free myself from this prison and embrace my femininity. That is the essence of my journey towards womanhood.

Writing emerged as the most powerful tool to showcase the lives of the hijras with sensitivity and compassion. Whatever affects the hijra community, also affects me personally. It was impossible for me to look the other way or keep quiet. Writing was the most effective tool to deal with the oppression. I had to write frankly and fearlessly about our lives that are lived perilously close to the edge.

There are several books written in English by people who have undergone sex change surgery abroad. But there were not many such books in Tamil, my first language. No other book, except the autobiography of Living Smile Vidya talked boldly about the lives of the hijras and the need to address the deadliness of the grave human rights violations we experience.

Meanwhile a deep personal crisis had a serious impact on me. I was disillusioned and wanted to quit my job at Sangama. I was also suicidal and wanted to end my life. My friends stood by me as pillars of strength and support.

They said to me, 'Are you mad? You are doing such good work for the hijra community. So many changes have taken place. You too have grown in the process. Try not to muddle your thoughts. See if you can do something more for the community.'

I found their advice sensible. I decided to take my mind off the disturbing event in my life and do something constructive instead. This decision led me to undertake a study on the lives of the hijra community and put down our experiences in the form of a book.

I see my role as a writer to be another dimension of my work as a human rights activist. Writing, for me, is a powerful way to connect the hijra community, my family and society. Through bridging the huge gap between these two worlds, I hope to initiate a dialogue; to make people see the interconnections; to underscore the fact that as humans we have to fulfil our sense of individual and collective responsibility. Writing, like any other art form, allows us to bridge yawning chasms. Art is a great unifier and leveller. It cements relationships. It holds the key to long-closed doors that have become rusty due to centuries of prejudice and ignorance.

In 2003, I took a one-year break from work to work on my first book *Unarvum Uruvamum* (*The Feelings and the Body*). Written originally in Tamil, it captured the experiences of 25 hijras whom I personally interviewed, and traced their journeys from childhood to adulthood. Most of the hijras whose stories appear in the book lived in Tamil Nadu; a few of them lived in Bengaluru. I did not want to present the book in an academic style but wanted moving, deeply personalized stories that emerged during the course of intimate conversations between my people and me.

Initially they were surprised that I would want to write about them. Many of them were genuinely puzzled. They said to me, 'Why do you want to write about us? What is the use?'

However, they were unanimous that I would be the best person to tell their stories for several reasons. According to them, only a hijra can truly understand hijras. They also believed that they could share their lives with me with openness and honesty that may not be possible for them with a person who was not a hijra. And lastly, they were certain that a hijra's unique perspectives about the community would enable a lot of unknown facts about the community to emerge and also clear myths and misconceptions about the community. I was touched by their faith and trust in me. Yet they had several doubts that they wished to clarify with me.

'Who is paying you? Will we get a share?' they asked me.

I patiently answered every question. Finally I said to them, 'Don't we have to change the stigma and discriminations that still persist about our community? Shouldn't we make people try to understand our emotions and feelings? This book is to make society understand that it is no fault of ours but a fault of society that we continue to lead such lives.'

I can never forget that moment. I saw joy and happiness on their faces. It was as if they had understood something that they had been struggling to understand all these years. It seemed as if a cloud had lifted from their view that had blocked the sunshine in their lives. From then on, each of the 25 people whose stories appear in the book shared their lives with me without any reservation. Even today when I recall how they wept while sharing their stories, my eyes fill with tears.

Until then, I thought that I was the only one to go through so much in life. But when I heard the stories of my community, many of them who had faced far more cruelty than me, all my suicidal tendencies vanished. It was a tonic that strengthened me and breathed new life into me.

Unarvum Uruvamum was translated into English as *Our Lives, Our Works: Telling Aravani Life Stories* and published by Yoda Press in Delhi. Later Yoda published it in Hindi as well. However, although the book was well received, I felt that there were several things missing. I realized that an in-depth narrative that captures the range of human rights violations experienced by the transgender community is possible only when the writer herself reflects on her own lived experiences rather than telling other people's stories based on formal interviews. Hence in 2007 I decided to write my memoir in Tamil. I was driven by a deep burning desire to tell my story.

I began to write and every time my pen grazed the surface of the paper, different episodes from my life flooded my brain like a torrential flashback. Over a period of three years, I wrote four drafts and every time I reworked it, a new incident would emerge that I would then weave into the narrative.

Bama, the well-known contemporary Tamil Dalit author, is an inspiration for me. When I read *Karukku*, her moving autobiography, it struck a responsive chord in me. Being a Dalit woman, Bama evocatively reflects on the multiple forms of oppressions and the discriminations that pursued her at every stage in her life. Was such an open honesty possible in writing? Bama's writing was something that I wanted to emulate. I longed to meet Bama. My wish was fulfilled when Loyola College in Chennai invited her for a book discussion on *Unarvum Uruvamum*. Knowing my admiration for Bama, they had invited her and wanted to give me a beautiful surprise. Four years later, we met again; as authors at the Jaipur and Hyderabad Literary Festivals as by then my memoir was published in English as *The Truth about Me*.

In the meanwhile, a review of the English translation of Unarvum *Uruvamum* appeared in *Tehelka* magazine in 2009. This led to a contract with Penguin Publishers for the English translation of my autobiography that I had written in Tamil. I insisted that V. Geetha, the well-known author, activist and feminist historian, translate my work into English. I was extremely satisfied with how the translation turned out. What impressed me was that the translator had retained my colloquial informal style, tone and voice in the English version.

The Truth about Me catapulted me into the international limelight. Overnight, I became a celebrity of sorts. Today, if you Google Revathi, it throws up several searches, and the book pops up first! I was overwhelmed when a publishing giant like Penguin approached me with the offer. I am aware that for most aspiring writers, this is a dream.

The book received popular and critical acclaim. Readers were unanimous that the book was a gripping read from start to finish. Although *The Truth about Me* was originally written in Tamil, it was first published in English. Everybody has their own memory, their own version of what happened. In my book, I talk about the intense physical and emotional abuse I experienced in my birth family because of my gender non-conformity. In *The Truth about Me*, I have spoken at length about such violations of children's rights in the birth family and also in the larger society at the hands of the state, rowdies and pimps. My family had no idea of the sexual violations I experienced. Besides, while I perceived their abuse of me as unfair, they believed that it was all for my own good; to make me mend my ways and live 'normally'. Hence I decided to first publish my story in English because no one in my family reads English and I wanted to avoid getting into trouble with them as by then, I was reunited with my family.

However, once the book was published, I became a media celebrity. Journalists interviewed me and when the articles began to appear in the media, my family and the hijra community came to know all about me. As expected, both of them reacted harshly to what they perceived as negative publicity (for them).

The hijra community was furious with me. They said to me, 'Why did you have to write everything so explicitly including the fact that you were raped? Are such lurid details necessary? Will a woman write like this? And you call yourself one! Will it not affect your family and show the community in bad light?'

My family too was unhappy with me. One of my brothers said to me, 'It's true that we beat you. We did so to make you mend your ways! And you go ahead and write all this!'

The hunger to write, to chronicle my life, became the purpose of my life. I wrote the book not to sensationalize or cause a scandal, but because I saw writing as a powerful tool in my activism and advocacy efforts to address some of the pressing concerns and needs of the hijra community, which faces a constant threat of erasure and marginalization. Incidentally the Tamil version of *The Truth about Me* was published as *Vellai Mozhi* in 2011.

Such reactions also made me think about the challenges faced by writers who happen to be women. If you are a woman are there only certain 'safe' topics you can write about without inviting censure from self-appointed guardians of public morality? For women writers, it seems that writing about taboo topics such as gender and sexuality, is a definite no. We don't have the freedom to hear our voices; to write our hearts out. Instead we write what society wants to hear. And sadly, some of us even begin to self-censor our voices.

However, as far as I am concerned, I find it difficult to subscribe to such double standards. And I have paid a huge price for my uncompromising stance on certain crucial issues. For example, I was an invited speaker at a seminar on legalizing sex work and to evolve a bill for the rights of sex workers. I spoke frankly about my own experiences as a sex worker and the gross human rights violations I experienced.

Later one of the faculty said to me, 'Was there any need for you to say that you were a sex worker? By all means, support sex work; but don't be confessional as it will tarnish your image!'

Ironically, I find such double standards distasteful. I gave up sex work when I joined Sangama. Even today, when my daily existence is precarious, I've chosen not to go back to sex work. It's a conscious decision on my part. Although my decision to give up sex work is highly personal, I support the rights of sex workers. Sadly, despite all the activism and seminars, society is unable to come to terms with sex workers as human beings with the same rights as the rest of society.

Today when I look back, I also realize that in my books I had articulated a traditional notion about women—focused on the 3Cs: cooking, cleaning and caring—be it children, husband or in-laws! But that was before I discovered feminism! I then realized how oppressive men have been towards women, forcing us to behave in stereotypically feminine ways—docile, obedient, modest and dress in saris and have long hair with flowers! I then understood how unfair it was. Today I dress in clothes that permit me mobility (salwar kameez, trousers and shirts) and have cut my hair short!

The Truth about Me was an eye opener for most people about the hidden lives of the hijra community. It has been translated into seven Indian languages (including Telugu, Malayalam, Kananda and Hindi) and also has appeared in e-book and audio book versions. It is also part of prescribed reading for a course in gender and sexuality in 300 colleges and universities across India.

Although all these have ben gratifying for me as an author, what I cherish most is the personal impact of the book. A woman contacted me after reading the book. She told me how meaningful it was for her to read my book as it helped her to come to terms with her daughter, who desired to live as a man. Today she is unconditionally supportive of her trans man son and has even arranged for him to undergo a Sexual Reassignment Surgery (SRS). Can there be any greater satisfaction than this?

The Truth about Me was launched by Penguin in New Delhi in 2010. Several eminent people from the publishing world and some of the organizers of the Jaipur Literature Festival (JLF) were also present. Later, I was one of the invited authors for the Jaipur Literature Festival in 2011. Urvashi Butalia, editor and publisher, Zubaan Books, was the anchor for the session.

At JLF, I met and interacted with several authors from across the world. I was delighted to be part of a gathering of such well-known authors. I was there for all the five days. I interacted with people in my not-so-fluent English! It was a proud moment for me when people wanted me to autograph the book, which also sold well! The language barrier hardly mattered. According to me, only a person with a peculiar sensibility and sensitivity becomes a writer.

During my session, I spoke in Hindi and Urvashi Butalia translated it in English. The hall overflowed with people and many of them were even seated on the floor! I forgot I was a transgender and instead felt I was a woman—and a powerful one that!

Sangama has played an important role in helping me blossom as a writer. The trainings, the grassroots experience and the ability to interact with people from different spheres of life was enriching and widened my perspectives. The same society that once ostracized me because of my hijra identity, today welcomes me with open arms!

Writing, I realized, was powerful to herald social change. Yet I wondered how many more Revathis, if they had such opportunities, would have emerged? Certainly, they would not have been forced into sex work. Perhaps they too could have blossomed as writers, artists and other professionals. This was the theme of my talk at the JLF. Differently gendered people don't need people's sympathy. What we do need is unconditional support that validates and recognizes our need to live our lives in accordance with our felt gender. I finally concluded that hijra rights are also human rights. I received a thunderous applause.

The Truth about Me forged a new grammar of writing. The intimate conversational tone of the book forged an instant connect with readers. Several authors also told me that I had broken established canons of writing and instead evolved a new idiom that was intensely personal and direct.

Writing the book was deeply cathartic and healing for me. During the process, my intense pain had been transformed into art. Isn't that the purpose/essence of creativity?

7

To Famila, with Love

In 2008, nearly eight years after joining Sangama as an office assistant, I rose to the position of a director. I was one of the five directors and was in charge of collectivization of the transgender community. However, the other two directors quit soon after their appointment and therefore I had to shoulder their responsibilities as well.

Sangama then had five branch offices in Bengaluru with a strength of 250 staff. I had no idea of my roles and responsibilities. However, I learnt on the job through trial and error. A year later, the organization appointed an assistant for me. Around this time I began to notice a strange shift in the attitude of the staff towards me. While earlier, assistants would hesitate to enter the director's room; they now just barged into my room as if it was a matter of right for them to do so! As I do not know to read and write English, I was dependent on the English speaking staff to translate the documents and emails from English to Tamil. Most often, they deliberately translated them incorrectly! Besides most of my time was spent in resolving conflicts between the transgender community and the Sangama staff.

However, despite all the struggles, I savoured several moments of triumph and success too during my tenure as a director. One of my unforgettable achievements was organizing advocacy campaigns and crisis intervention for Shilpa, a trans woman who was subjected to brutal police harassment on false charges.

Even before I became the director I had witnessed the premature death of several promising initiatives. One such instance was the formation of Vividha, a collective for non-English speaking gender and sexual minorities. One of my saddest moments was the break up of Vividha in 2003 because of conflicts among the members and between the transgender community and Sangama staff. It was painful for me to watch the crisis in Vividha that led finally to its break up. Personally it was like the death of a dream because we had dreamt of an autonomous identity for Vividha. However, post Vividha, we believed that dependency on external funding would be the death knell for the activism we believed in. Hence, through Sangama, we began to build the capacity of the transgender community to form collectives or community based organizations (CBOs). These included Samara, which provided HIV-related services; Karnataka Sexual Minorities Forum, which focused on legal literacy and advocacy; LESBIT, which focused on advocacy for lesbians, bisexuals and trans persons; Sadhana, which enabled HIV positive people to access government benefits; and the Sex Worker's Union that championed legalization of sex work.

At this point, I was reminded of an observation by Babasaheb Dr B.R. Ambedkar in Agra on March 18, 1956. 'There is some progress on education in our society. By acquiring education, some people have reached to the higher positions; but these educated people have deceived me. I was hoping from them that after acquiring higher education they will serve the society; but what I am seeing is that a crowd of small and big clerks has gathered around, who are busy feeding themselves and their families.'

Similarly once people from the transgender community get into good positions in an organization, they begin to behave like members of the non-transgender community! This was one of the main reasons Vividha broke up. Besides there was extensive internal politics within Vividha. For example, members were divided on issues such as who experienced more violations with law enforcing agencies—trans women, kothis or trans men?

However, my views were entirely different. I believe that we are who we are. Being a transgender is all about who you are deep inside, not how you appear on the outside. Whether we call ourselves male to female trans persons, female to male trans persons, gender queer, we have to negotiate our transitions and our place in the world and struggle against oppression.

I mention all this because one of the most successful initiatives organized by Vividha was the Hijra Habba festival, which was conducted on a grand scale in 2003. The Hijra Habba affirmed the principle that hijras are lawful citizens of the country whose fundamental human rights (including civil, political, economic and cultural rights) need to be protected and guaranteed through the law and by meaningful engagement with the government, civil society and the general public.

Famila, my chela, played a major role in successfully organizing this festival. Famila was a natural leader. She was a graduate, spoke excellent English and was well dressed, her favourite being Western clothes. Dark, dusky and beautiful, with an enviable hour glass figure, Famila was stunningly good looking. When she walked into a room, heads turned towards her. She had a certain compelling presence that was impossible to ignore. Although I find it difficult to pinpoint what exactly was the essence of Famila's universal appeal, she exuded a certain sense of elegance and grace.

Articulate and forthright in her views, Famila was a passionate activist for the rights of gender and sexual minorities. With her exceptional communication and fund raising skills, she mobilized over 2000 people to attend the programme, and collected donations from the general public to organize the festival.

Famila was a person for whom life was never black and white; it only had several shades of grey. For example, while as a feminist she disliked beauty pageants because they portrayed women negatively, she had no problem in participating in beauty pageants for hijras in the annual Koovagam festival.

'Mummy! At least now they will know that even hijras look beautiful! And that we can do many things other than just sex work and begging!' she said to me.

Although Famila was my chela, in reality we were like a mother and daughter who shared a close relationship and a rare friendship. She disliked hypocrisy. Her life was an open book. Famila identified herself as a hijra, bisexual and a feminist. In the early years of Sangama, Famila was also a board member of the organization, and a project coordinator for hijras and transgender people.

Famila lived her life based on the principles she believed in. Her life was her message. Through principles and practice, she challenged the norms of a hetero patriarchal society that she felt was oppressive and unfair not only to women but to people who were of different gender and sexual orientation. She was the first person from the transgender community, who without fear or hesitation told the media that she was also a sex worker.

I must confess that until I met Famila, I was ashamed of being a sex worker and felt guilty and ashamed about it. But Famila helped me to realize that by subscribing to such negative stereotypes, I was indulging in self-hatred and discrimination—the very aspects of mainstream society that I was trying to address through my advocacy.

'I am a voluntary sex worker. It's our choice. We are not coerced or forced into it,' she declared to the media and in open fora. Famila made me realize and accept that sex work is also a profession. Even after she joined Sangama, she continued with sex work.

What impressed me most about Famila was that her passionate activism for sexual and gender minorities was based as much on her own lived experiences as on mature insights into gender and sexuality, which she acquired by attending the one-week intensive residential programme on gender and sexuality conducted by the Sexuality, Gender and Rights Institute, held at Pune in 2003.

Famila's home was an open house that overflowed with every denomination of sexual and gender minority people. She firmly believed that non English speaking sexual and gender minorities needed an articulate spokesperson for their cause and she took the initiative to create a space for them and enable their voices to be heard and their needs and concerns to be addressed. She did sex work to support her large family whose members seemed to increase with every passing day. She was the first person from the hijra community who openly supported female to male trans persons or trans men. She used her fluency in English and her strong communication skills to champion the cause of the non-English speaking sexual and gender minorities.

This was something that even I did not expect her to do. Because even within the hijra community, female to male trans persons are not accepted, they are treated with contempt and scorn.

'Can you produce a baby? Show us your penis and then we will talk about whether you are real men!' the elders and other members jeered at them.

But Famila was made of sterner stuff.

'Do you have a uterus? That doesn't prevent you from thinking that you are women!' she famously retorted.

She openly confronted such people and what she considered to be outdated values and attitudes. Although she identified herself as hijra, she was accepting of different sexual and gender identities, especially female to male trans persons. Through her outspoken activism and her fearless articulation of the rights of people of marginalized sexual and gender identities, she spearheaded a new brand of activism. Famila opened my eyes to the possibility of a truly inclusive world. She taught me that even if our ideals appear like a mirage that is no reason to stop pursuing them. For this and for many other such beautiful insights, I am indebted to my Famila. She was acutely aware of the several dilemmas in my personal and professional lives. Firmly but lovingly, she helped me to realize that although it is easy to run away from a situation; it requires great courage to engage with distressing situations, confront them and emerge stronger in the process.

Famila was a source of solace and strength to me. I recall that when I was going though a grave personal crisis and often felt suicidal, Famila gave me courage to rebuild my shattered life and look forward to a future with optimism and hope. There was nothing I did not share with her. She knew my highs and lows; my dreams and desires; my shadows and fears. Famila was a radical in every sense of the term. She was in love with a trans man and the two of them were determined to get married.

'Mummy! We will create history of sorts. It will be the first such marriage in India between two trans persons,' Famila told me. I could sense her joy and happiness about her impending marriage. At that point, Famila was working towards getting civic identity cards such as voter ID and ration cards both for herself and her trans man partner before formalizing the marriage. Famila was a woman in love and was open and expressive about her feelings.

However, around this time in 2003, things became difficult for Famila at Sangama. The organization brought in a rule that Sangama staff should not do sex work after office hours as they were apprehensive of the police foisting false charges on them. Famila, however, believed that choosing to do sex work was a matter of right; her prerogative. She firmly believed that she was a person first and her role as a staff of the organization was only secondary to who she was. She argued that people in other professions also regularly did secondary businesses and her involvement in sex work was also similar to that.

However, the organization refused to relent and finally a frustrated Famila had no other option but to resign from Sangama. Ironically, despite Famila's tireless crusade for the legalization of sex work and the rights of sex workers, even feminist organizations denied her support and space.

After she was cut off from Sangama, she felt marooned and unanchored, as if her lifeline had been cut off. To compensate, she began to indulge in full time sex work. I suspect that it began to take a heavy toll on her health, both physically and psychologically. However, Famila put up a strong façade and even I, who was closest to her, did not suspect what she was going through.

Some time in the first week of July 2004, Famila telephoned me. There was little in her voice to suggest the deep psychological turmoil that was raging inside her.

'Mummy! Tell me the recipe for radish chutney!' she said to me.

I gave her the recipe. Little did I realize that it was the last time I would hear her voice.

A week later, several senior staff at Sangama were attending a public hearing in Bengaluru. As it was late in the night, we decided to stay back in the home of one of our colleagues. Around midnight of July 17, 2004, I got a phone call from Famila's partner who said that Famila committed suicide by hanging herself.

My world stopped. I was numb and did not know how to react. My colleagues and I rushed to the hospital where Famila was taken.

I saw her body in the mortuary. Dressed in black chemise and tights, Famila looked as if she were sleeping. When I touched her body, it felt warm. Perhaps life still flickered in her. I pleaded with the doctors to revive her as I felt that there still was hope for my Famila. But my pleas fell on deaf ears.

Famila was just 24 years old. A life full of promise had been nipped in the bud. At her funeral, I performed all that had to be done. I wept because it should have been she who had to be doing this for me and instead now she had given me this heart-breaking task. Her parents and brother had come for her funeral. Her father, who had cut off all ties with her, was weeping openly. If only he had accepted Famila, welcomed her back into the family fold, and not cared about society, his daughter would probably have been alive today. However, I felt that each of us individually and collectively were responsible for Famila's premature death—her family, friends, Sangama, her partners and even me.

Five years after Famila's death, I too resigned from Sangama because of ideological differences. It was not possible for me to watch people profess something noble publicly and behave in the opposite way in private. Perhaps that's why I go through so much pain and turmoil. It's impossible for me to put up pretences; to play politics. I know I have paid a huge price for what most people would consider 'silly and stupid values'. Many have also taunted me that I don't know how to survive in this world. But that's who I am. It's impossible for me to be otherwise.

Leaving Sangama was a bold decision, although it was not impulsive. It meant giving up a job that assured me a fixed salary every month. I was at yet another crossroads of my life. I was certain I did not want to go back to sex work. What I wanted to do was to live my life as an independent activist for the rights of sexual and gender minorities. Like an answer to a prayer, I received a one-year fellowship from Samvada, a Bengaluru-based human rights organization, to research on female to male trans persons.

I miss you, Famila. Every moment. You certainly would have been a source of great strength and support had you been alive. You sparked the fire of activism in me. Today, I am doing all that you dreamt of. I offer them to you in gratitude and deep appreciation of the phenomenal woman you were.

8

Criminalized by Law

On July 2, 2007, the Delhi High Court delivered a judgment that challenged the 150-year-old IPC (Indian Penal Code) Section 377, and in the process decriminalized same sex relationships. The judgment generated a euphoric response from certain sections of the LGBT (lesbian, gay, bisexual and transgender) community as well as from the larger society. Never before had a judgment made such media headlines and a topic of conversation for all. For several days, news channels buzzed with news of this judgment.

Section 377 of the IPC was drafted by Lord TB Macaulay, British historian and politician, and enacted in 1860 during colonial rule. Reflecting morally conservative Victorian values, it criminalized all sexual acts, consensual or non consensual, that did not lead to procreation and criminalized people who indulged in non penetrative penile-vaginal sex.

Under a sub chapter titled 'Unnatural offences', it reads: 'Whoever voluntarily has carnal intercourse against the order of nature with any man, woman or animal, shall be punished with imprisonment for life, or with imprisonment of either description for a term which may extend to ten years, and shall also be liable to fine.'

The law has been used to address cases of child sexual abuse. And I support the use of laws to prevent sexual abuse of minors. However, this law has been used to criminalize same sex love between consenting adults as well. And this is where the law becomes unconstitutional, hampering the right of individuals to equality.

In the earliest reported case of *Queen Empress Vs. Khairati* in 1884, we see that it is a hijra or a person seen as male who was found dressing in female clothes who was criminalized. She/he was found dancing in women's clothes in the village and was medically examined. The medical examination report stated that the person was used to having anal sex and this activity criminalized him/her. Historically, laws have always been used to criminalize the more marginalized and visible amongst us. In this case, it's always trans people who are at the receiving end of a disproportionately large amount of violence from the state.

In 1993, a relatively unknown NGO, the AIDS Bedhbhav Virodhi Andolan (ABVA), launched a public appeal for the repeal of this oppressive law. The next year, the first legal challenge against the law emerged when ABVA filed a petition in the Delhi High Court against the antiquated law on the grounds that it blatantly violated the constitutional rights of life, liberty and non discrimination. The context of this legal battle was the denial of permission by the Delhi police to ABVA activists to distribute condoms in Tihar Jail in Delhi. According to them, as the jail was gender segregated, distributing condoms would imply abetting a criminal act as perceived by 377 IPC. The case, however, dragged on for several years and when it finally came up for hearing, it was dismissed because by then the ABVA had become defunct.

Meanwhile, across the country, there was a spike in incidents of police harassment of same sex people, especially homosexuals, in several Indian cities. In 2001, two instances of attacks in Lucknow, popularly known as the 'Lucknow incidents', one on homosexuals in a park and the other, an attack on the offices of an NGO working on safe sex issues, triggered a number of events that led to a long legal battle. At this point, Naz Foundation, a Delhi-based NGO that works on HIV/AIDS outreach and interventions with the men who have sex with men (MSM) community, and the Lawyers Collective (lawyers for Naz Foundation), filed a Public Interest Litigation (PIL) in the Delhi High Court in 2011 against this law.

An eminent two-judge bench of the Delhi High Court that comprised Chief Justice A.P. Shah and Justice S. Muralidhar heard the case. The judges finally ruled that criminalization of consensual sex between adults in private violates the Constitution's guarantees of dignity, equality, privacy and freedom from discrimination based on sexual orientation. They bolstered their arguments on the grounds that 'there is almost unanimous medical and psychiatric opinion that homosexuality is not a disease or disorder but just another expression of human sexuality.' They referred to the fact that homosexuality was declassified as 'abnormality' or pathology in the Diagnostic and Statistical Manual (DSM) of Mental Health in 1973 after a rigorous review of medial evidence that proved conclusively that it is not 'deviance, abnormality or pathology'. Thus the judges 'read down' Section 377 so that it decriminalized sexual orientation and consensual sex between same sex individuals in private. However, the judges ruled that Section 377 will continue to govern cases of non-consensual sex between adults as well as sex with children.

There were several petitions that were filed against the judgment by religious groups. On December 11, 2013, the Supreme Court of India, in a major setback for gay rights in the country, set aside the 2009 judgment of the Delhi High Court. In its judgment the Supreme Court bench of judges, G. S. Singhvi and S. J. Mukhopadhaya stated that very few cases have been registered under Section 377 and stated that it criminalized acts and not identities.

One has to have experienced being victimized by IPC 377 to realize how negatively this judgment impacts people like us. According to it, oral and anal sex is regarded as 'unnatural', while only penetrative penile-vaginal sex is considered 'natural'. However, applying the same logic, I often argue that even oral and anal sex between heterosexual married couples is 'unnatural'. But that ironically is considered a 'private' matter and is never discussed. Instead to our dismay, we find that the morality lens is focused on the transgender community.

Even the campaign against Section 377 fights for the right of private, consensual sex between adults. But for street based hijras for whom privacy itself is inaccessible, what protection will we get even if this is decriminalized?

As a transgender person, I—like other members of my community—have to satisfy my bodily hunger for sex. How can we satisfy our sexual hunger? Only by having sex with men in public places? Can we get married to men? No. Society brands our sexual desires as 'wrong'. This makes me question the very basis of what is 'normal' and 'abnormal'.

Some trans women feel that we experience ourselves as complete women only when we have sex with a man. Not just if we wear saris, wash vessels and make kolam or rangoli! For us, the fulfilment of our lives as women is if we are able to give and receive love in a physical relationship with a man. Sex is like food. It is a biological need for men, women and animals. We feel desire for men. Because we don't get partners very easily, sometimes, we look for sex in sex work. So the state says we must have safe sex but the same state says that certain kinds of sex are criminal. I firmly believe that what is normal and what is abnormal is just a perception.

Perhaps one reason why oral and anal sex are termed 'unnatural' is that society views only heterosexuality as 'natural' because according to this view, sex is meant only for procreation. I question this very basis because to me it rests on shaky logic. If giving birth is 'natural', then contraception is also 'unnatural' because it is against nature. But then we conveniently turn a blind eye to such ethical issues. If sex is only for reproduction, then don't use contraception. Birth sex, education and experiences do not necessarily determine one's gender identity. Rather, they are also based on personal choices and how one feels deep inside.

Sadly, most parents, teachers, lawyers and health care professionals lack the sensitivity and maturity to understand such a complex issue. They continue to regard sex and sexuality as something 'shameful' and 'sinful' and are unwilling to discuss these openly with their children. Had my family and teachers been supportive of my gender identity when I was a child, my life would have been radically different. I could the have stayed with my family, completed my education and perhaps found a suitable employment. All this would have built my self-esteem and enabled me to lead a life of dignity and respect. At any rate, I would not have internalized a sense of shame and guilt that because of my 'different' gender identity I am 'abnormal', 'deviant' or 'dirty'.

Forcing a person who is attracted to someone of the same sex, to be attracted to the opposite sex, is a violation of the human rights of that person: each human being's sexual orientation is a matter of individual choice. In a heteronormative society that thinks that there are only two genders (man and woman) and that heterosexuality or sexual relations between man and woman, are the norm, oral and anal sex is a taboo. Forced sexual intercourse is rape. I too was raped anally by a rowdy in an urban slum in Mumbai. My guru took me to a doctor nearby. The doctor did not even examine me. He simply interrogated me, 'Why do you have anal sex? Can't you be like a woman?'

Most doctors write a prescription for some kind of ointment and callously dismiss us. So we resort to home remedies because of the excruciating pain. The anal region is an extremely soft and sensitive region where all the nerve endings in our bodies converge. I would sit in basin of warm water to which I would add Dettol. The throbbing pain would resume when the water cooled.

Even when women in marriages have some issues, they can access doctors if they have money or support from home. Doctors know how to treat gynaecological problems. But in the case of trans men and trans women we do not have the option to access treatment even if we somehow manage the money for it. The first hurdle is the prejudice of the doctors when they see us.

Anal sex is common even among heterosexual couples. Sometimes, one partner, usually the husband, seeks it from a sex worker. But for some people, anal sex gives as much pleasure as vaginal sex. This is something I've always highlighted in my activism, to not judge other's choices and desires. However, because of my rape I am hesitant and fearful about anal sex. Probably if I had a less painful and careful initiation into anal sex, I too would have enjoyed it.

When one has sex in a safe space, one can use lubricants. But trans women, who are involved in street-based sex work, are forced to hurriedly indulge in oral or anal sex in public spaces with little or no privacy. We are always afraid of being rounded up or picked up by the police for such 'criminal' behaviour. But if we have to satisfy our urges or earn money, we have no other choice. What if someone sees us? So we do it quickly and furtively. Under such circumstances mishaps such as anal tears are common.

However, because anal sex is a taboo, we are unable to seek treatment for anal sex related problems. The medical community is not sensitive to our concerns. Even in the jamaat (the social organization in the hijra community) we cannot share it. It becomes a subject of ridicule and contempt and we are the laughing stock. 'Oh! You know she was torn during anal sex!' and such knowledge becomes public. This is a gross violation of privacy.

However, today, sexual and gender different people are vocal and articulate about our needs and desires. Yet doctors and lawyers continue to stigmatize and brand oral and anal sex as 'unnatural'. There is a lot of judgment on their part. Unfortunately, such a view has gained widespread acceptance because law, religion and custom also support it. It is erroneously believed that same sex desire is a Western phenomenon and therefore contrary to our 'lofty' Indian culture and tradition.

The stark truth is that same sex desire is not a Western phenomenon. It is a human phenomenon across cultures. *Kama Sutra*, the world's first treatise on sex, was written by Vatsyayana, an Indian sage, over 4500 years ago. The book also talks about same sex desires as 'natural' and describes oral and anal sex between same sex couples.

Do gay people consider hetero sex as abnormal? Then why are they being targeted? Is *Kama Sutra* then a sham and a lie? Look at the erotic carvings in our temples, which convey the message that such desires are not disease or deviance but perfectly normal.

But it is not only Section 377 that is used to criminalize us. There are several other laws that do not get as much attention from mainstream media and the LGBT movement that are used routinely to target trans women. The Immoral Trafficking Prevention Act is of course a major one. It is not actually used by the police to stop trafficking of young girls and women but to target vulnerable women in sex work. Hijras who are street based sex workers are targeted a lot under this. We are very visible when we are in public. Everyone knows we are hijras. So the police target us. They often use laws against public nuisance on us. Are we also not humans? Do we not have constitutional rights too?

On November 25, 2014, 200 hijras were picked up and put in the infamous Beggar's Colony near Magadi Road in Bangalore under the Karnataka Prohibition of Beggary Act 1975. Even hijras who were not begging but going to the market to buy provisions for their houses were picked up. Just being a hijra is criminal under law, it seems! No employment opportunities are given to us and when we do the two jobs that are available to us—sex work and begging—we are punished for it! Laws that are meant to protect us instead criminalize us. What is the way out of this for us?

Unless and until we are open about gender, sex and sexuality, we will be shrouding them in shame, secrecy and silence. Sexuality education should be introduced in schools so that teenage pregnancies can be avoided, and there is more awareness and acceptance for non heterosexual desires. We do not have any right to stop any two people who love each other, whether they are homosexual or heterosexual, from being with each other. Sex is only one part of life, it is only one expression of companionship, it is something that needs to be accepted and fought for in order to live a life of human dignity. Gender expression or gender identity is also a matter of a person's choice. Laws that criminalize gender identities and sexual orientation have no place in a democracy and must be struck down. Everyone must join hands to fight for equal rights for all of us to live in a just society.

A few days back, many news channels called to ask me about the U.S Supreme Court legalizing same sex marriage. I was asked about the effects of the decision here. I said that in Namakkal district, just this week on June 24, 2015, the body of 21-year-old Dalit youth,

Gokulraj, was found on railways tracks near Anangur. Just like Ilavarasan was killed and found on the railway tracks in Dharmapuri, Gokulraj was also murdered on suspicion of an inter-caste affair. How can I talk about same sex marriage in the U.S when even heterosexual couples don't have the right to marry and love beyond caste here?

For us to be liberated from gender oppression, we must also be liberated from caste, race, and religious oppression. Our struggle must be against all these systems of power and not just one.

9

A Momentous Decision

I joined Sangama in 2000 and worked there for ten long years. I became the director in 2009. The Sangama Board of Trustees felt that as the organization was widening the scope of its activities, they needed three directors to assume independent responsibility of each of its major initiatives. One director was in charge of services; another of advocacy and I was in charge of collectivization of sexual and gender minorities.

The other two directors resigned their jobs within a month of assuming charge. I did not know why. As a result, I had to shoulder their responsibilities as well. Sangama has always identified itself as an organization working for the human rights of the working class, non-English speaking, sexual and gender minorities. Hence the fact that they chose me, a working class, non-English speaking trans woman as director, was a matter of pride for me.

I was in charge of five collectives: Samara (HIV/AIDS for sexual minorities), Karnataka Sexual Minorities Forum (advocacy, policy change and legal awareness), Sex Workers' Union (female sex workers and sex workers belonging to sexual and gender minorities), Sadhaney (accessing government welfare schemes for people living with HIV/AIDS), and LESBIT (lesbian bisexual women, female to male trans persons, intersex and transgender). For all these collectives, I had to oversee the capacity building of the organizations to look at the preparedness of the staff to assume leadership roles including finance management and legal requirements, fund raising and liaising with funding agencies.

As a non-English speaking trans woman who suddenly found herself in a leadership role, it was a challenge. Yet I was determined to rise to the occasion. According to me, although I was designated as director, I strongly believed that we had to work as a non-hierarchical team, where everyone was well informed and efficient. Organizational hierarchy, I believed, was something just on paper; for accounting purposes and donor accountability. For instance, if there was a visitor to Sangama, I believed that it was not just one person's responsibility to introduce Sangama. I believed that everyone from the office assistant to the director could and should take ownership. Perhaps such a perspective gave me the confidence that as a lone director I could ably guide the organization.

However, to my dismay, I realized it was not so simple. There were 250 staff members for the five collectives and they were overseen by an administrative structure that monitored their work and progress. Although each collective had a coordinator, I had to oversee their functioning. The previous directors of Sangama were either not community members or were

English speaking members who belonged to sexual minority communities.

I noticed that Sangama staff behaved with a certain degree of propriety and decorum with the earlier directors. They were well behaved with them and respected boundaries. However, with me, they were very different. They would storm into my cabin and argue endlessly with me, often in very rude and offensive language. They demanded prompt promotions, increases in salaries and crowded my working hours with endless demands and trivial things, which they could have handled themselves.

I was not upset with Sangama staff. As a trans woman, I know the pain of sexual and gender minorities. Of course, some of their demands were reasonable. For example, someone who had worked in the organization for seven years was overlooked for promotion and a colleague who had recently joined was favoured. But I wondered why the earlier directors had not addressed such problems. There were crisis interventions, follow up work and new proposals to be prepared for donor agencies as the earlier projects had phased out.

The Shilpa crisis was the biggest challenge I faced as director. It was unprecedented. Sangama's reputation as an organization committed to the human rights of gender minorities was at stake. There were big players involved such as the law enforcing agencies and corporate health care providers. Most importantly, the transgender community could be further stigmatized if the case didn't go in our favour.

Because I did not know English, I had to depend on English speaking office staff in the organization, to translate emails into Tamil or Kannada. I had to beg and plead with them to cooperate with me. They looked down upon me still as an office assistant. I felt that they did not respect me as a director.

In such hostile circumstances how could I continue as the director? All funds were closed at that time, we had to write new proposals for funds. On one occasion, we had to organize an event hosted by two of the Sangama collectives. We had to find out a source of funding, plan the focus of the event, finalize the programme schedule and plan the guest list. But the staff would go to earlier directors and completely change everything. I wondered if I were just a token director! I was bewildered by such internal office politics and conflicts. If people still wanted to have a say in the internal functioning of an organization, why did they pretend to quit at all, only to micro manage from outside? I could never understand such messy office politics.

Sangama hand-held Samara for seven years, providing it much needed technical support, help with fundraising, administrative support and advocacy. We now felt that the child had grown and it could walk, and so we decided to let them walk independently. All that they needed was to get an FCRA (Foreign Contribution Regulation Act) certification that would authorize them to get funds from abroad. Samara members too wanted to be independent organizationally: they wanted only for technical support from us. However, although many of the staff secretly supported the handover, some of them expressed their displeasure. I realized, to my dismay, that this was all part of a double game, so common in NGO politics.

Meanwhile, during my tenure as director, funding proposals were written and even approved by funders.

I felt it was time I moved on. After all, it had been ten long years. I wrote a 20-page letter to the Board of Trustees of Sangama outlining the reasons for my decision to part ways with the organization: non cooperation of staff, my difficulties, office politics, and interference by one of the previous directors. I gave my resignation letter with the stipulated three-months notice. The Board did not ask me why I was leaving. They did not invite me to talk things out with them either.

I recall an organizational vision building workshop for Sangama in which we explored six values sacred to an organizational culture: sacrifice, confidentiality, democracy, team spirit, proactiveness and equality. I had followed every one of these sacred principles. But did the people around me follow them? This caused me great anguish. We say that we work for the non-English speaking working class, for sexual and gender minorities. But I realized that as a director you are respected only if you are upper class and English speaking.

The decision to quit Sangama was most painful for me. I am aware that many people say that Sangama was responsible for my growth. Although I accept that, it is equally true that Revathi was also instrumental in Sangama's amazing growth and development as an organization.

As everywhere, it's only people who cause problems. Their internal squabbles and power games tired me out. After a decade in the organization, I wanted to make space for the second line of leadership. I therefore quit in 2000.

Once again I found myself at a crossroads. Sangama had been a lifeline for me. Now, at 42, I found myself with no job and no support system. I was firm that I did not want to go back to street-based sex work because its violation of bodily integrity was repugnant to me. Similarly I found street-based begging to be equally demeaning. Faced with such a dilemma, I even wondered if I should end my life. Interested as I was in social struggles and working for social change, I did not like the idea of continuing with sex work. Ironically even if I left my activism behind, it refused to leave me! But then I knew fully well that there was no money in activism!

The future loomed over my life in great uncertainty. I began to wonder if at the end of it all, I would be faced with no other option but to return to sex work and begging for the rest of my life. But as I grew older, I realized I would not be able to do that either.

I returned to my home in Namakkal. Even when I was with Sangama, I often visited my family. My father had divided the property equally between my brothers and sister. My brothers, who are lorry drivers, were living independently with their families. When I returned, my siblings heaved a sigh of relief as from then on there would be someone to look after my father.

My relationship with my father is purely transactional. I take care of him and in return he provides me shelter. Like most men, my father too has a sense of male entitlement. As a woman, he expects me to take care of him. It almost seems like it is a matter of right. At times I feel that I am his domestic help, not his daughter! All this of course, only reminds me of the secondary status of women in India. Now that I too am a woman, how could I expect it to be any different for me?

Therefore I decided to put up with all the adjustments my new life demanded. For both of us, it is just a matter of convenience. Even though I was treated like a domestic help, at least I had a roof over my head. Otherwise, I do not think I would have survived the ordeal and lived to tell this story.

The most difficult part of the transition was the loss of a regular monthly salary. I was unsuccessful in finding suitable employment opportunities in nearby Namakkal. And now that the responsibility of looking after my father was mine, I could not go elsewhere for work. My source of financial and emotional sustenance was the aravani jamaat, a social structure that is unique to the hijra community. My gurus and chelas rallied around me in a touching show of solidarity.

Maniyamma, my guru, supported me financially every now and then. Even now when I visit Bengaluru, I stay at my chela's house. I don't go to anyone else's house. No former staff of Sangama who worked me ever called me and checked on me or enquired about me. Nobody respected me because of my being a trans woman. Noori, my chela, helps me with money, booking tickets and other things. I don't know when I will repay her, but she says that I have through my activism helped others a lot. She works in a catering unit to support people like me. A trans man, who is like a son to me, helps me with written work. I get emotional support from my trans family.

When I took up activism, I left the hijra jammat system saying I didn't need it any longer. But now, I feel that it is to this system that I have come back for support. Because I have acceptance to a certain extent from family, and a few friends, I am surviving.

But because a lot of people don't have these, a lot of trans people are lost to suicides.

My Nayak from Hyderabad died in a fire accident in Nand Nagri in North East Delhi in 2011. More than 50 hijras were injured in the fire and 15 hijra gurus died. Very few news reports highlighted this. The fire engines took a long time to come to the spot. I heard that several members of the general public stole jewellery instead of helping the hijras while the fire raged on. The Delhi government announced a compensation of ₹2 lakhs each for the hijras who died and their families. But does the government recognize our hijra families? I am yet to hear of a single compensation handed out for this tragedy. Do our lives have no value at all? Nobody protested against this either. It seems that whether in mainstream or alternate spaces, hijra lives are not worth the time or attention of others.

Meanwhile, I received a one-year fellowship to research the lives of female to male trans persons from Samvada, a Bengaluru-based organization that works with youth. This was a ray of hope for me. I received a monthly stipend of ₹10,000.

Researching the lives of female to male trans persons was deeply meaningful for me. I felt I was carrying forward Famila's legacy and her vision that embraced diverse sexual and gender minorities. Even among the transgender community, female to male trans persons are not accepted because the community feels that they are not 'real men'. My writing and activism were powerful tools to address such negative stereotypes and discriminatory attitudes. My life now had a newfound sense of purpose and passion. Over time, I had built relationships with these men as their mother. Most of them left their homes or were thrown out when they were very young. I filled the void left by their families in their lives to a certain extent. Protected in the pages of their mother's story, they venture to tell their stories for the first time.

10

Life as Performance

I discovered another way of taking my life and work to people—through performance. Whether it is writing or acting (the latter is something I have recently discovered), my initiatives in these areas were driven by a burning desire for social change.

In 2004, Santosh Sivan, the well-known Tamil film director and cinematographer contacted me for a film he was making. Centered on the transgender community in Tamil Nadu, the film *Navarasa* was being shot during the annual Koothandavar festival at Koovagam village near Villupuram in Tamil Nadu. Sivan wanted me to scout for a 19–20 year old transgender person to play the central character and also wanted me to do a cameo. I identified Kushboo, a transgender who plays the central character in the film. The film won the national award for the best Tamil film in 2005.

My favourite scene in the film is the one where a journalist at the beauty pageant quizzes me on trivial things like my favourite colour, favourite dress and so on. I use the opportunity to engage meaningfully with him. Although he is annoyed with me for what he perceives as my brashness, I nevertheless try to enable him to see us for who we really are—survivors of birth family violence, mocked at by peers, ridiculed by teachers at school and hounded and hunted by the police—just because our gender identity does not match our physiology.

'Have you ever been beaten with a cricket bat because you wanted to live as a woman? Have you ever been thrown out of your home and not knowing where else to go, landed at the jammat? We need to wash our stomachs, don't we? What else can we do except begging and street based sex work?'

There is a stunned silence. The journalist is speechless.

My role in *Navarasa* led to another commercial Tamil film *Thenavattu* (Lethargy), by Tamil film director V V Kathir, released in 2007. I play the role of a transgender leader who has a heart of gold. Bollywood actor Poonam Bajwa and well known Tamil actor Jeeva played the lead roles. V V Kathir had interviewed several trans women for this role but was not satisfied. He then saw my performance in *Navarasa,* and felt that I was the person he was searching for. Sadly, my trans women friends in Chennai were reluctant to divulge my contact details. But he was resourceful enough to track me down.

Kathir invited me for a meeting to discuss the story and characterization. I was apprehensive for several reasons. As an activist I strongly disapprove of the portrayal of transgender people in commercial films. We are there just to provide comic relief or are portrayed as 'dangerous criminals'. But Kathir reassured me that while my concerns were valid, the portrayal of the trans woman character in this film would be different.

He kept his word. Not only he, but the entire crew, including lead actors Poonam and Jeeva were friendly and treated me with unfailing love and courtesy. In fact they called me 'amma' (mother). In one scene, where actor Jeeva had to rush towards me and scoop a dying me in his arms, his legs hurt me accidentally. He was profusely apologetic and constantly enquired if I was all right.

Acting in this film was a novel experience for me. For the first time, I got an idea of what goes into the making of a film—lighting, camera angles, make up, costumes and dialogues. The film was particularly memorable for me because I play a trans woman who acts as a bridge between the trans community and the non trans community and actually unites the lovers.

According to several of my friends and well wishers, the film was an eye opener for them. Even today I blush in embarrassment when a flicker of recognition lights up people's faces in Tamil Nadu when they see me.

'Did you act in *Thenavattu*?' they ask.

'Yes', I reply, smiling like a star.

My only regret is that I wanted to play the role of a woman in a film. That has not happened so far.

In 2012, *The Truth about Me* was translated into Kannada as *Badaku Bayalu* by Du Saraswati, well-known Kannada author. In 2013, Dr M Ganesh, activist and faculty from Ninasam Theatre Institute, Shimoga, Karnataka, read *Badaku Bayalu* and was moved by my story. His friend Rajini Garuda from Dharwad, Karnataka, had gifted him a copy of the book. He thought that it was a powerful narrative to perform on stage. Janamanadatta, his 11-member theatre group, uses theatre as an instrument for social activism. They staged *Badaku Bayalu* and invited me for the forty-ninth show of the play.

In 2013, the community staff of Sangama offered to organize a show of this play and went to see the rehearsal in Heggodu in Sagar district. They demanded that the scene in which they were talking about my love life, marriage and other personal aspects of my life should be removed before they organized the show. The director Dr M Ganesh called me and asked me about this. He told me that Sangama was not ready to organize the show if they didn't take that scene out. I refused to cut the scene. So we decided to sell tickets and stage the show independently. Several people, both trans men and trans women women helped me sell tickets and organize this independently. I do not see people as staff or political opponents. I see everyone as people from my community. It is very unfortunate that marginalized communities are always split because of such politics.

I was stunned when I saw the performance of the play finally. I had taken four years to write my story. And yet how could they so marvellously recreate the story of my life in just one and half hours? I felt like I was watching a movie. My story was so seamlessly woven together. It was a surreal experience.

The actors had not even met me at that time. They had just seen a photo of me. Actors Vineet and Chandran, who played Revathi in various stages of my life, lived the role. They were completely in tune with my feelings. I then realized that this was pure art. They had not merely read the book but identified completely with me.

I was choked with emotion. My body was shaking. I wanted to scream loudly. But I somehow controlled myself in order not to disturb them. People who were sitting next to me were holding my hand because they saw how I was affected. While watching the play, tears welled up in my eyes. I relived the multiple traumas in my life—harassment by family, friends, society and police. Emotions seethed inside me like a turbulent ocean. At the end of the play, I was overwhelmed by the emotions I had buried away inside me. In a sense I felt more pain when I saw the difficult scenes of my life than I had felt when they were happening to me in reality.

The Janamanadatta team does not do theatre for the sake of money. They do shows on various social issues. They charge only for travel, food and the production costs of the shows. They have a 13-member crew. I was struck by NGOs taking funds and making tall claims to work for media sensitization and this theatre group's silent and powerful work to bring awareness on social issues. I was impressed by their activism through art. It touched people's hearts more than any speeches or public programmes. Theatre has the power to move people in a way that conventional activism does not.

Dr M Ganesh wanted to do a different play after the 50th show. After one week, I called him and said, 'Sir, we can change a lot of things through this play. Many trans people and their parents will watch it. We must stage 50 more shows.'

He agreed to this. I expressed my desire to act in the play, although I had no formal training. I wanted to meet people and interact with them in all the villages they were touring. Dr Ganesh and his colleagues were supportive of my desire. I underwent a two-month training at Ninasam Theatre Institute. I was thrilled at the possibility of acting. In my mind, I thought I would act like Shivaji Ganesan, and B Saroja Devi, both leading yesteryear stalwarts of Tamil films. Frankly, I think I over acted then. Dr Ganesh said to me,

'Chandran is not Revathi. He has to act as you. But you are not acting, you just have to be Revathi.'

Yet during rehearsals, I found it difficult to just be myself! Acting was easier! And every time I 'acted,' Dr Ganesh would gently remind me, 'Be yourself!'

I stayed with Dr Ganesh in his house. His wife and kids were accepting of me. In fact, his wife was so touched after reading my story that she is the one who had requested him to stage my life as a play. Dr Ganesh had a Kinetic Honda on which I would take their kids to school. I felt very happy being part of their family.

This experience taught me that if at all we get acceptance from any section of society, it is from people who have felt the pain of exclusion. Even if we look for houses, it is only in slums that we find space. Even in most of the villages where shows were organized, they were done by small groups.

Karnataka is a ranga bhoomi—there is such a vibrant theatre movement in this culturally and artistically rich state. We received a standing ovation at the end of the 50th show. Many people from the audience had tears in their eyes.

They came up and spoke to me. They said, 'We had no idea about transgender people and your lives. All we knew was that you beg on the streets! When we were young, our parents would scare us by saying, "If you are naughty, I will had you over to a transgender who will take you away to Bombay and make you beg!"

Your story has really opened our eyes to the realities of your lives!'

Their reactions touched me. I felt humbled. Despite having worked for over a decade at Sangama, I felt that art has a powerful and far greater reach and appeal than NGO work. I developed a newfound respect for art and its role as an instrument of social change.

In many places, the audience refused to get up and leave after the play. They wanted to hear me speak after the show. A lot of people said that they had many negative stereotypes about us. Only after seeing the play, they said that they were opening their hearts and minds to the issues of trans people.

We went to more than 30 districts of Karnataka with this play. In some places, they put us up at government guest houses. In smaller villages, they would arrange places for us to stay in schools. In Shimoga, the chairman of a college came to me and said, 'If anyone in your community wants to study in college, please send them to me. I will give them free education, hostel, food and other facilities.' I told many trans people about this opportunity but nobody has taken it yet. The fact that he came forward with this offer was a big success for me.

Chandran who was acting my role was called 'chinna' (small) Revathi. I was called 'periya' (big) Revathi. For two years he didn't cut his hair to act as me. Heggodu is a hilly village where the monsoon is heavy. The Ninasam Institute was surrounded by thick forest. Chandru would always catch snakes. He caught at least eight snakes, played with them and then released them in the forest. But he was very scared of injections and would scream if you took him to a doctor. I really enjoyed my time with them.

They called me 'akka' (elder sister) and I really felt that I had a family when I was with them. In many places we would stage my play and in some others, they would stage a play on Babasaheb Ambedkar. Usually, they stage plays on anti-caste issues. For the first time, Manjamma, a jogappa, or a member of the transgender sect in Karnataka and Andhra, did many performances in the Mohini role in the Ranga Bhoomi. I was the first trans woman to play this role. In some places, women came up on stage and slipped bangles onto my hands.

They said, 'We accept you as one of us.' I felt deeply touched by their response.

If we didn't get plays organized by someone else or a group on one day, then all the expenses would have to be borne by the theatre group . We would ask schools to organize but most of the time it would be vacations. We would take the book *Baduku Bayulu* in the van everywhere with us and after the show, many people would buy the book from us.

A lot of trans people are interested in folk art and performance like Karagattam, Mayilattam, Vayilaattam, street plays, koothu and other folk art forms. In fact, trans people for the first time came in large numbers to watch my play at Ranga Bhoomi.

So much money is spent on NGOs and HIV funding. Why can't the government support such cultural expressions of marginalized communities? It would really help in initiating social change. The biggest challenge to theatre and its survival is television serials and feature films. I now wish to do the play in Tamil. I want to continue touring with Ganesh and his team. But my age and health do not permit me to do so. No NGO who supposedly works for trans people helped in organizing any of this. Only some trans friends independently helped me in my efforts.

Since then Janamandatta has staged 87 shows of our play. Our last performance was on March 8, in Bengaluru, on Women's Day. The show was organized by the Women and Child Welfare Department, Karnataka. A few positive changes are happening in Karnataka in the depiction of trans people in theatre and films. For example, this year the national award for the best actor was won by Sanchari Vijay in his role as Vidya in the film *Naanu Avanalla Avalu* based on Living Smile Vidya's life. Incidentally, the director Mr B S Lingadevaru had discussions with Janamanadatta during the shooting of his film. Currently Janamanadatta is staging a play on Jotiba and Savitribai Phule called *Satyashodak*.

And so, I discovered from this life-changing experience that far away from the limelight and the media attention so many small groups are doing such great work quietly, without drawing attention to themselves. It is these endeavours that we must support because they are the ones who are actually working for change.

11

Finding My Sons

I would like to recall the famous story of Shikhandi[1] from the *Mahabharata*. Princess Amba was the eldest daughter of the King of Kasi. She had two sisters, Ambika and Ambalika. Amba was secretly in love with Shalva, the king of a neighbouring kingdom, and wanted to marry him. On the day of her Swayamvara, when she was planning to chose Shalva as her husband, Bhishma, the famous warrior from Hastinapur, abducted all three princesses as brides for his half-brother Vichitravirya.

Amba, already in love with another man, frankly confessed her love to Vichitravirya, who let her go back to Shalva and instead married her two sisters. However, to her great disappointment and sorrow, Shalva rejected her as she had been touched by another man. In desperation, Amba went back to Vichitravirya and begged him to marry her. He, however, stubbornly, refused, as 'a gift once given cannot be taken back.'

[1] Devdutt Pattanaik (2014): *Shikhandi, and Other Tales They Don't Tell You* New Delhi: Zubaan/Penguin.

Increasingly desperate, she begged Bhishma to marry her. However, he was bound by his vow of celibacy. Instead he encouraged her to go back to her father or remain in the palace as a maid.

A furious Amba swore to take revenge on Bhishma. She was later reborn as Shikhandi, the daughter of King Drupada. Drupada, who had prayed for a son, was disappointed that he had a daughter. But to make up for his disappointment, he raised his daughter as a son and even got him married. Thanks to a yaksha, who exchanged his manhood with Shikhandi, he was even able to fulfil his conjugal role as a husband. Later in the Kurukshetra war, Shikhandi, stationed in front of Arjuna, shot arrows that killed Bhishma. The latter surrendered, as he knew that Shikhandi was a woman in an earlier birth and as a Kshatriya, he would not fight a woman. Shikhandi is the earliest example of a trans man or a female to male trans person. The Sangam literature also talks of trans women.

Trans women or male to female trans persons are known by various names and gender identities in different parts of the country: hjira, thirunangai, jogti, shiva shakthi, ardhanari, and kinnar. Although they have been abandoned by their families, they continue to live in social units known as jamaat, which mimic the family structure. The jamaat is similar to an extended family and, like a household, is headed by an elder known as the guru who in turn adopts a set of chelas or disciples who are like daughters to her. For such gender non-conforming children, who later become trans women, the jamaat becomes their lifeline and security.

Besides the government and NGOs have launched targeted HIV interventions for trans women or male to female trans persons. However, today the most common livelihood options for us include street based sex work and begging, badhai (child birth, new beginnings, weddings), folk dances, cooking, and since the 1990s, jobs in the NGO space. Over the years, several trans women have distinguished themselves in various spheres. They include: Narthaki Nataraj and Ponni (Bharatanatyam), Priya Babu (activism and writing), Kalki (activism and media), Living Smile Vidya (activism, theatre and writing), Swapna (government service), Grace Banu (engineering), Gunavanthy (security guard services), Padmini Prakash (media), Bharathi (church services), Asha Bharathi, Sudha, Bharathi Kannamma, Sheetal, Sankari, Aruna, Jeeva, Nooriamma and many others. Not only are they fine professionals and prominent transgender activists, they have also emerged as strong voices for the community, highlighting their needs and concerns in the mainstream.

Despite the widespread stigma and discrimination experienced by trans women, the existence of supportive spaces and structures such as the jamaat and NGOs working in HIV/AIDS prevention is something that is not there for trans men or female to male trans persons. Trans women identify themselves as female while being raised in a gender (male) that does not match their chosen gender identity. Trans men, on the other hand, identity themselves as male, though they are raised as a gender (female) that does not match their chosen gender identity. The fact that they are biologically female makes them more vulnerable to sexual harassment and this persistent fear makes it more difficult for them to leave their families.

A trans man I know faced a peculiar predicament. When he applied for the post of a salesgirl in a showroom, the employer asked him why he was dressed like a man. Instead he insisted that if he grew his hair and wore a sari, he would get the job! That a single person seen as a woman can find it difficult to live independently is not something that I need to tell you. Working class non-English speaking trans men are burdened by their lack of knowledge of English. Sometimes such people are married off even before the idea that they are men crystallizes.

I once stayed with a trans man friend who lived in Kerala. He lived independently, worked in a juice shop and has even rented a house saying that he is male. He cut his hair, and dressed in trousers and shirts. He has not had surgery. Although he has completed his graduation, he is unable to find a job. He is not permitted to use the girl's toilet. His only option is to use the men's toilet. But as there are no doors and he cannot stand to pee in men's urinals, it is extremely difficult for him. Hence he frequently withholds urine and empties his bladder only when he is certain that he will 'not be caught with his pants down'.

Like others of his community, my trans man friend binds his chest with crepe bandage or cloth to make it flat. He then layers it with t-shirts and shirts. He is willing to go through all this and more because of a deep burning desire to live as a man. He even introduces me as his 'Mummy'! His ID proof however, shows his legal gender as female. Because of this discrepancy between appearance and name, it is difficult for people like him to find houses on rent and jobs.

Trans women are more visible. But this does not mean that we can erase or deny the existence of trans men. After *The Truth about Me* was published, and it became prescribed reading for a course on gender studies in several colleges and universities in the country, I took the opportunity to talk about trans men. Unfailingly, every student and teacher asked me in surprise: 'Do such people also exist? We want to know more about trans men.'

Even in the transgender community, trans men are not accepted. That's because of gender stereotypes that are so prevalent in our society. We commonly believe that a woman is defined by breasts and a vagina; a man by his penis, beard and moustache.

The hijra community says, 'We have removed our moustache, beard and penis. We are complete women. Even if they (trans men) wear men's clothes, can they be called men? They might remove their breasts, but if their ovaries and uteruses are there, they can become pregnant. And can they just wear briefs and stand around like men?'

I question this very notion of boxing men and women into such neatly defined exclusive categories. Devara Dasimayya, the mystic Kannada poet, says, 'Breasts and long hair—is this a woman? Beard and moustache—is this a man? But what of the soul, which is neither man nor woman?'

Female to male trans persons or trans men are often forced into marriages. Many commit suicide because of the absence of support systems, even in the NGO space. In the hijra community, we have kinship systems in the form of the jamaat. There is no denying the support and solace the jamaat provides us. But unfortunately, there is nothing like this for trans men. Besides they find it difficult to find female partners.

While I was with the crisis intervention wing of Sangama, I had the opportunity to counsel several trans men for whom Sangama was the only refuge. Listening to their stories full of pain and turmoil made me realize that I needed to highlight their needs and concerns too. A one-year fellowship from Samvada gave me the opportunity to do 12 in-depth interviews with trans men.

Phalloplasty or sex reassignment surgery for trans men is too expensive for working class trans men. Hence most of them undergo bilateral mastectomy and are on hormone therapy. We are now lobbying for the fact that this is sufficient for them to be considered men.

My research on trans men is but a small initiative to create awareness about this invisible sexual minority. My trans men friends regard me as their 'amma.' I always talk about trans men in all public discussions. Despite all the support from the jamaat, my journey towards womanhood was a struggle for me. I don't want my trans men sons to go through such pain.

I capture here five lives of trans men who share their stories with me with honesty and courage. Each story is unique in its own way. For instance, we have Mookan, a poor uneducated Dalit trans man in a remote village near Salem in Tamil Nadu. Like many people in his village, he too is a migrant agricultural labourer. A friend once told me about him. I tracked him patiently and luckily, he was open enough to share the story of his life with me.

There are many people like Mookan who struggle with their gender and sexuality. Utterly confused, and bowing to the dictates of society, they lead a troubled double life. Their lives are anonymous. The Mookan I know cannot be found today. He left his village and I have no idea where he is. Yet I am still trying to trace him and hope that one day I'll find him.

Like him, there are many Mookans whose lives are caught between two different bodies and feelings. I still believe that one day I will meet him.

We then have the story of Charu and Karthika. Classmates in school, they developed a strong attraction for each other at a young age. Their love sustained itself through a troubled adolescence and adulthood and respective marriages to men. Yet they were unable to get over their desire and passion for each other. It was so strong that after being reunited years later, they decide to step out of their marriages because the joy of being together was more meaningful for them than being trapped in a heterosexual marriage in which they were not happy

Society permits only one kind of love—heterosexual love between a man and woman, bound by caste, class and religion. Even the law is supportive only of heterosexuality. But a human being can get attracted to anyone across gender, caste and religion.

And then we have the story of Kiran and Radhika. Kiran, who copes with the multiple oppressions of having a disability and being a trans man. He runs an NGO for people with disabilities and is an activist for the rights of gender and sexual minorities. Today Radhika and Kiran are still happily married and have been for over ten years. Their journey continues despite the insults and hardship of everyday life.

Then we have Sonu, a trans man who was Famila's partner. They were all set to marry when Famila's tragic suicide cut short the dream. Famila was a great support for him. Today, he has transitioned and become a man and works for people like himself.

Christy is one of the first trans men I met in my activism. His story is unique because he was raised by a trans woman who didn't accept him as a man till the end of her life. His story shows us that trans women too need to learn to accept and love our sons and brothers. He now lives with his partner and is a leader and role model for many others.

I have spent many years with female to male transgenders (FTMs) and have tried to understand their lives. Each of these five men sat with me and shared their stories. I then wrote all the stories in Tamil which was then translated into English.

Then we have Satya and Gee who have been generous enough to accept my request to write their own stories and send them to me. Gee also read, back translated into local languages each one of these stories to edit them all with his brothers and sent them to me. He dislikes me thanking him for it, but thank you my son for all the hard work and time.

And now, let us hear their stories in their words.

12

Fatherhood

There was never any doubt in my mind that I am a man. Sadly, I am a man trapped in a woman's body. I had known this all along, even when I was a child.

Whenever there was a fire in the town, I ran with the men to douse the flames. Along with them, I climbed onto the wall and took buckets of water from the women. I hitched up my sari and petticoat like a man would do with his lungi, tied a bandana around my head and helped to douse the fire.

A fire mishap occurred in my neighbour Rasamma's house. Her daughter was studying in college. One day, the daughter hugged and kissed me. I felt thrilled at the physical intimacy. Although I put out the fire in her house, Rasamma's daughter's kiss kindled a fire in my body. The flame of that desire still burns within me. Nothing has doused that. I cannot live without seeing her.

I dreamt that I was Sarath Kumar (a popular hero in Tamil films), and she was Jyothika (a popular heroine in Tamil films in the 1990s). My love began to thrive on such fantasies. Yet, this was a closely guarded secret in my mind, No one knew about it. I did not even tell that girl how I felt about her.

How could I? I too was seen as a woman. Moreover, I am an uneducated dalit. She is an upper caste, educated girl. But I was unable to forget her. I did not tell her that I was in love with her. Instead, I kept my feelings bottled up inside me. Was there any point in nourishing such romantic fantasies for another girl? I stifled my desires and instead focused on my work and family.

Even though I dressed like a woman in a sari, blouse and petticoat, I wanted to wear a komanam (an inner loincloth worn by men in south India) and work in the fields! So I would tuck my sari between my legs, pull in the pleats and push the fabric into the waistband of my sari at the back, and plough the fields, draw water, cut sugarcane, plant paddy, cut paddy, and thresh grain using bullocks. When I did all this labour, I felt like a man.

The people in the village often said that if Rakkamma (as I was known) removed her nose ring, her earrings, if she cut her hair and wore a lungi and shirt, she would be a man! But because they said this, I didn't feel ashamed or anxious. Instead, I'd say, 'Why don't you get me the lungi and shirt and I'll wear them,' and I would continue with my work.

However, even if women do as much work as men, they do not get the wages men are paid. In our village, a man who works as an agricultural labourer is paid ₹120 every day, while a woman gets only ₹70. Being seen as a woman, I too was paid only ₹70. Unlike most other women, I do not swing my hips seductively and gossip about others. I worked like a bull. Actually there is no difference between a bull and me in terms of physical strength and endurance.

As I am the eldest of three sisters, all family responsibilities fell on me. I felt overburdened. I felt angry with my father who died because he drank too much.

Appaen kudichu kudichu kundi vadichu sethu taarunga!

My father's arse exploded because he drank too much!

My mother was sick at the time. She worked as an agricultural labourer and brought us all up. I think that it was a great achievement for her, considering the difficult circumstances of our lives. You know, life is very tough for a female-headed household, especially in rural areas. Why, even the street dogs barked at us, as we had no male protection.

My sisters refused to study beyond class 5, although we tried our best to make them go to school. Finally, we gave up as they adamantly refused despite our best efforts. Our mother's health did not improve even though she was getting medical treatment.

My alcoholic father had left us with only a fallow piece of land and a thatched hut. It was agricultural land that was entirely dependent on rain. But whether it rains or not, we can't survive by pinning all our hopes on the pottai kaadu or fallow land. So, we work as agricultural labourers on other people's land as well. Should I feel happy that he at least left us with this? Or should we worry that if there is no rain we will not be able to cultivate maize, millet or groundnuts?

My parents had four daughters. Couldn't I have been a boy? At least I would have got more wages. And then my mother and sisters would also have had a man to protect them and guard the house. Even now, *I* guard the house! But sadly, I am not paid a man's wages at work!

As far as I can remember, I was always the man of the house. I would get into the water well holding on to a thick rope and repair the motor. If the house leaked during the rain, I would thatch it. I climbed palm trees and plucked nungu (palm fruit) for my sisters. I climbed coconut and palm trees, fermented toddy and got it down. I enjoyed doing all these 'manly' activities. But what I detested were feminine chores like making kolam (a traditional floral design in South India made with rice flour), sweeping and cooking!

My mother usually asked me to cook if she was unwell. I was, and still am, a clumsy cook. My mother was angry with me because I did not cook well.

'If she stirs the earthen pot with a ladle, it will break and the rice will fall into the fire!' my mother taunted me.

On another occasion she said, 'You are as old as a donkey, but don't know to cook rice!'

My mother was worried about what people would think of her.

'In your husband's house, they will say, "Look, how she had brought up her daughter!" They will all talk ill of me.'

I was fuming with anger. I hated even the thought of a husband. Because *I am* a man.

Edu thodappa kattaiya! Pursuhan irushan!

I threatened to take the broom. I was angry at even the mention of a husband.

'Don't you ever say that you will get me married or send me to my husband's house! If you do that, I will not ever consider you my mother!'

I argued endlessly with my mother. How could she even think of getting me married?

'You got married to a drunkard. He gave you four kids and he too has gone! Don't you ever dream that I too will get married and have four children like you!'

I detest the scent of a man. In fact, I detest anything to do with men.

'If you want to get me married and drive me out, all of you will suffer for food!' I threatened my mother.

As far as I was concerned, I was the man of the house. When my drunkard father passed away, I automatically took over his role as the head of the family.

'If you want to get a son-in-law, get your two other girls married and satisfy your desire! Don't drag me into your plans!' I told my mother. Thankfully from that day onwards until today, no one in my home has ever asked me to get married.

***

My younger sister was 17 years. We got her married to my mother's aunt's son. She began to live independently with her new family. In the meanwhile, we began to look for an alliance for my second sister. But she turned down every proposal. She insisted that she would get married only if I got married.

'What is the connection between my marriage and yours? My responsibility is to get you married. Our father was useless. Don't worry about me. Short or tall, if it's a good family, get married. Otherwise you will have to suffer doing coolie jobs with me. Clean, cook and stay here if you want!'

One day, she ran away with a neighbouring boy! I could not believe that this was the girl who had wanted me to get married. He was an upper caste boy.

His mother lamented, 'She has tempted my boy and taken him away!'

The people in the village said that as the girl is from a lower caste, the couple should not be allowed to enter the village. If they did so, they would be killed. My family was poor and from a lower caste. So we could not confront them. But I did not give up.

'Even if my sister took him away, why did he go? Is he a small, milk-sucking baby? What justice is this?' I argued.

'What do you know? Nothing except to climb palm trees like a man and ferment toddy! What would you know about any of the things women do? You can neither be included among men or women!' People in the village taunted me.

Amma also tried to silence me. She warned me to hold my tongue. Sadly my mother did not support my sister. As far as she was concerned, if she comes, even if you cut her up and kill her, we will not question you!' she promised them.

Both my sister and the boy ran away because they liked each other. How could society and my mother pass such a judgment on them? Can't people who love each other make a life for themselves? What did they do wrong? Can't we just let them be? My mother and people of the village did not like my views. We did not know anything about the whereabouts of my sister who had eloped. We wondered where she was, how she was.

I am known as 'vayadi rakkama' or the argumentative Rakamma. People said I was so argumentative that I would have made an excellent lawyer!

I was confused about my identity. Who am I? In appearance I am a woman. But my feelings are those of man. Is this right or wrong? How should I behave? Do I behave the way society wants me—like a woman? Or do I behave in accordance with how I feel? Like a man.

***

For three months in summer, the heat was scorching. The monsoon failed once again. We could not do any cultivation. The earth was dry, parched and huge cracks were visible on the surface. The parched earth was a metaphor for my life as well, waiting for relief.

My mother had an incurable illness. One day, suddenly, she died and with that all her sufferings came to an end. I wonder if my sister who eloped even knew about our mother's death. She did not come for the funeral. A few relatives and people from the village attended just for the sake of a formality.

My youngest sister was eight years old. Even though I did not know how to cook, I made her kanji (gruel). I had no work, and there was no money. Do I search for my sister whose whereabouts I am clueless about, or do I protect this vulnerable child? I was in a dilemma. I had no one to turn to for support. At the same time, no one was concerned about my problems or me.

I wanted to protect at least my honour. I decided to change my appearance to that of a man. So I cut my hair, wore a lungi, and a shirt and gave myself a name: Mookan. I went to another village in search of work. I became the father of my youngest sister.

I was always afraid that people would know I'm biologically a woman. I was upset about the sudden uprooting in my life. Would I get work as Mookan? How would I work with a child? What would happen to our thatched house and the fallow land when I went to another village for work? Will anyone deprive us of even these meagre belongings?

Grumbling about my life, I nevertheless wandered in search of work. Even if I got work, I would not get a place to stay. Also, in a new village, nobody called me to work because they did not know anything about me—about my family, about me, where I came from, and my caste.

I begged for food to feed my child (my sister). Although I was capable of working in the fields as an agricultural labourer, I could not get a job. What's the use? This god has made me beg! What sin have I committed? I was shattered. I did not know where I was going or what I should do.

My little sister and I walked towards Kombai village in Kollimalai hills near Salem. We saw a pumpset in a field and both of us bathed. I drank the water and thought, 'Shall I jump into the well with the child? Alas! I know to swim, so even suicide was not an option for me!'

The owner of the field spotted me.

'Yaaru da! Who are you? What are you doing here?' he shouted at me.

'Sami! Lord! I am from Mohanur village.'

I then told him my story.

He still did not believe I was biologically a woman. He was certain that I was a man. And he was also certain that I was a kidnapper. Alarmed, he called other people nearby.

'Tie him up! Kill him! The truth will come out!'

I shrank into myself like a criminal. If the child had not been there, I would have got beaten up. Luckily for me, one of the men in the village had married a woman in my village, Mohanur. He called his wife and asked her to find out about me. When she made enquiries, it became obvious that I was telling the truth.

'Go back! Even if you are dressed as a man, nobody will give you work if they do not know you. They will be suspicious of you. If they know you are a woman, will they let you live?' the landlord said to me.

He gave me a hundred rupees and asked me to go back to my village.

I took the money. I walked on holding the hand of my little sister, my child, towards an uncertain future.

Revathi has been unable to trace Mookan after he shared his story with her. She hopes he is living happily as a man with his sister and hopes to find him in the future.

13

A Love Against All Odds

I was born in Puducherry, in Tamil Nadu. My father brewed illicit liquor. My mother is a homemaker. I am the youngest in a family of four siblings—two elder brothers and an elder sister.

A few years after I was born, our family migrated to Rasipuram (near Salem in Tamil Nadu) because of poverty. I joined an elementary school there. My elder sister got married when I was in Class 5. My mother began to work as a construction labourer. My father meanwhile got a job in the handloom weaving sector as a supervisor.

I studied up to class 12 or second PUC (pre university college) as it is often called. I was not interested in studies. Although I was raised as a girl, I preferred to play sports like cricket, kabbadi and volleyball. I always won the first place in sports. When I was in class 5, I had a classmate called Lalitha. If she did not come to school, I missed her terribly and longed to see her.

We lived in a small village near Rasipuram. The village school admitted students only until Class 5 and for further classes we had to go the nearby town. I came of age when I was studying in class 9. I could sense a lot of physical and psychological changes within me. I became attracted to the girls in my class. At first I was confused by such feelings and could not understand what was happening to me. I knew how a girl was expected to behave. But feeling attracted to girls, I wondered if I were a boy. But I am not a boy. Or am I? At that time, it didn't even cross my mind that I could become a man.

Lalitha was not with me in class 6 as she had joined another school. I did not like one of my classmates, Karthika, in the beginning. I disliked talking to her. Strangely, perhaps it was because of not talking to her, I began to love her. Or maybe I didn't talk to her much because I liked her. In any case, I felt scared to tell her that I was attracted to her. I felt it was 'wrong'.

One day, despite myself, I confessed my love to her. She did not say anything to me. I pursued her, and kept telling her about my love for her. I imagined myself to be a man while talking to her. But with other girls, I behaved like a girl. Because I felt shy and unsure about my romantic attraction to girls, I was unable to talk like a man with other girls. But I don't know why, I thought of myself as a boy only while talking to Karthika. I did not know if it was 'right' or 'wrong' to feel this way but I liked her a lot.

Ten days later, she gave me a slip of paper and asked me to go somewhere alone and read it. I read it all by myself in the bathroom. She had scrawled, 'I love you' in it! I kissed the paper. My heart felt like a fluttering butterfly that wanted to dance from the earth to the sky! I felt that I was born anew and I tingled with this newfound sensation. I felt joyful. Ecstatic. But both of us hardly talked in class.

Karthika would go into the bathroom when no one was around. I would follow her. We would express our love openly there. One day some of the other girls saw us go into the bathroom together. They laughed at us us. But one girl said, 'Keep quiet! Maybe she has some secret problem in her private parts. That's why they are going there together!'

We found that comforting. I began to visit her home as a friend. We both had kept a diary together. We both wrote in it and took turns keeping it with us. She left it at home and came to school. Her mother read it.

***

Her mother called me home and said to me, 'Why have you written in her diary romantically like a boy. This is not proper behaviour!'

I became scared. We belonged to different castes. She was upper caste and belonged to a well off family. We belonged to the same sex. I was afraid of the consequences. I fell at her mother's feet and begged forgiveness. I said that I had done it in ignorance.

Her mother said to me sternly, 'Don't be friends with my daughter. Please don't come home and don't ever let me catch you talking to her.'

When Karthika and I were in Classes 9 and 10 respectively, we did not talk to each other because we were afraid of our families. Ours was a co-educational school. Girls were not supposed to talk with boys. If they did, they were punished. We played together, boys and girls, during the games period. That was permissible because it was sports. During the games period, I moved with boys without any reservation, as if they were my brothers. Earlier girls could wear churidhars during games. I too wore only that. Then I began to wear shorts. Girls would make fun of me for wearing boys' clothes. I felt shy. In spite of these questions, we were serious only about who won or lost the game.

By then her mother had complained to my teachers and my family about the diary she had found. Even the headmaster knew about it. He warned me to stop doing all this. Karthika's mother enrolled her in another school for Class 11. We could no longer meet each other. As Karthika failed in Class 12, her family decided that she would stay at home. Soon, they got her forcibly married. Our happiness and love for each other was all too fleeting and short lived.

Karthika's mother repeatedly warned her, Charu (me) is not a good girl. Her behaviour is unacceptable.'

She thus successfully manipulated Karthika's mind with all such accusations about me and got her married. I was unable to meet Karthika. It was impossible for me to attend or stop her marriage.

***

Meanwhile, I was unable to study after Class 12 because of my family's financial situation. I was also unable to concentrate on my studies, as I was constantly thinking of Karthika. So, I got a job in a music shop. Gradually, I began to explore the town on my two wheeler, hoping to find out where Karthika lived.

Siva, who worked in a neighbouring tailoring shop, was a good male friend who understood and acknowledged my feelings. In the beginning, Siva was in love with me. But when I told him of my true feelings and identity as a man, he became a good friend. He consoled me and gave me a lot of support and comfort. I was put in charge of the music CD shop. The owner rarely visited the shop. I found solace in my loneliness. But whenever I thought of Karthika, I became disturbed. Desperate, I listened to several old Tamil songs. My longing for her became more intense with time.

'Where is she? How is she? Is she also pining like me? What troubles is she facing?' Every day I would be tortured by thoughts of her. I felt haunted by her memories.

My voice and Karthika's voice sounded similar over the phone. Many people mistook one for the other when they heard either of us. Karthika's father died when she was young. I had heard from my neighbours that her grandmother was not happy with Karthika's marriage.

***

I thought of a clever plan. I telephoned her grandmother who mistook me for Karthika. I decided that this would be the best way to find out about Karthika.

'Patti (grandmother), did you get my letter?'

'Yes. I got it.'

Patti's response gave me a lot of courage.

'Can you read out the letter to me. I've forgotten what I wrote,' I fumbled.

'Why ma, don't you remember what you wrote? Why do you ask? Do you have any problem?'

'Nothing like that, Patti. I just asked.'

'You haven't replied to my question. You did not call me up or come to visit me,' Patti said.

'You wrote that you live in Karur and even gave me your phone number. I don't talk to your mother and neither does she talk to me. After my son died and she got you married against my wishes, we cut off relations. You have married your mother's brother. If I have contact with you and your husband informs your mother she will say, "This old lady has no other work!" I don't wish to have anything to do with her but then why does she jump like Kali and accuse me of wanting to see my grand daughter? Now you know why I did not want any contact with you,' continued Patti.

'How are you? Happy with your husband?' she asked.

'I am fine. Give me my phone number, Patti.'

'Yennadi amma! What is this, amma! But how can you forget your own number?'

'Yes, but I've forgotten it now. I am unable to tell the number if someone asks. Please give it to me.'

Patti gave me the number.

'Thanks, Patti. I will call another day.'

***

It was two years since I had heard Karthika's voice. I called her on the phone.

'Hello?'

Immediately I recognized her voice.

I was unable to speak.

'Hello? Hello?' I heard a voice at the other end.

'Karthi, its me Charu,' I answered hesitantly in a feeble voice.

She banged the phone down.

I was hesitant to call again. I was in a dilemma.

Why did she cut me off despite knowing who it was? Was her husband at home then? Perhaps her mother or some other family member was around. A lot of questions arose in my mind. Despite Karthika's behaviour, I desperately wanted to call her again and talk to her. I trembled with the impulse to telephone her again.

I resolved my inner anxieties and called. Even before she said, 'Hello' I said, 'Karthi, this is Charu. I want to talk to you. Please don't cut the line.'

'Look here! Don't you have any sense? Why are you calling me? How did you get my number? Hang up this phone call. Or I will tell my mother,' she screamed and banged the phone down in anger.

***

I had been searching and longing for her for the past two years, I wanted at least hear her voice. Yet she did not understand my feelings. I was hurt by her behaviour. I was overwhelmed by emotions and felt tired.

It was enough for me to know she was happy. That's all I wanted. So, once again I called her.

'Where are you calling from?' she asked.

'From the Music Centre in Rasipuram,' I said and gave her the address.

'I will come there with my husband.'

My heart was fluttering. Will she come to the shop with her husband and create a scene? Worried about the possible consequences of her visit, I shut down the shop early and went home.

The next morning I opened the shop. Thankfully, so far there was no problem. Something told me that

Karthika would still love to talk to me but because of the circumstances of her life she was unable to do so.

Once again I telephoned her. She picked up the phone on the first ring. It seemed as if she had been waiting beside the phone for my call.

'See, Karthi! Don't hang up the phone. I am not calling to bother you. Be happy wherever you are. I don't wish to spoil your life. Please don't misunderstand me.'

Even then she was not prepared to talk to me. She banged the receiver down.

I did not call her back. I was worried that I would cause her problems.

***

I was unable to focus on work and eat normally. I was like a mad person. My parents came to know about this. They wondered why I was not eating well and sleeping normally. They sensed that something had upset me. They came up with what they perceived as a solution: If they got me married, everything would be fine. So, they fixed a matrimonial alliance for me!

I tried my best to convince them that I did not want to marry.

'Look! Your two brothers are married, they have kids and live like good householders. You are now 18 years old. We should also get you married, this would fulfill our responsibilities,' they reasoned with me and finally fixed my marriage.

On the day of my engagement, Karthi telephoned another classmate Priya, who lived close by. Priya told her about my engagement.

'Ask Charu to call me up. She called me several times but I could not talk to her because my mother was with me. Today she is not with me, so we can talk if she calls,' Karthi said to Priya.

Priya passed on the message to me. The engagement took place that day and so I could not call her. But I telephoned her the next day. She talked patiently.

'Priya told me that you are engaged.'

'Yes! A marriage in which I am not interested. What can I do? I have no other way out. I don't know what is in your mind. If you say yes to our relationship, I will stop this marriage.'

'I still have a lot of love for you. I am unable to forget you. What can we do if we keep thinking of this world and our family? We have to resign ourselves to our fate and carry on. We can't defy our families and live together. We are born as females, will society allow us to live together? Be happy wherever you are,' she said and hung up the phone.

I thought what she said made sense. Why did God create us as female, give us such love for each other and play with our lives? Who can change this? What can we do? I was deeply worried and felt hopeless.

***

I got married. I then went to my in-laws place for the first time. The phone rang. My father in law looked at me and said, 'From now on, this is your home. Your world; your universe. You have to look after all this. Answer the phone.'

I felt apprehensive. Who could it be? Would it be Karthi? How would she know my number? In this state of confusion, I answered the phone. It was for my husband. His friends were congratulating him on the marriage.

Neither Karthi nor I ever wanted to elope. Ours was a pointless, meaningless love. If you are a girl, you have to marry a boy and vice versa. Who can change that?

After marriage, a woman's life is bound by a lot of dos and don'ts. Girls are brought up to be good girls who will later make good wives and good daughters-in-law, and good mothers. Ours was a joint family. My life was no exception. I was expected to talk sweetly to my husband, get along well with him, be a wife to him and please him in every possible way. But I had no interest in all such wifely duties and obligations.

My husband had no bad habits like drinking and smoking. But he was suspicious of me. He constantly suspected my lack of affection towards him. Is there another man in her life? Ironically when I myself am a man, he suspected another man in my life! He forced me to have sex with him although I had no interest. He would search our bedroom for any tell tale signs of my suspected male lover. He would beat me and exhort me to get more dowry from my mother. My father-in-law too began to torture me for dowry.

As my husband and I often fought with each other, I would run away to my mother's place.

'Whatever happens you must stay with your husband,' my mother said to me and always forced me to return to my husband's family.

Even though I did not desire it, I was forced to satisfy my husband sexually. I was unable to voice my distress. Every day was a living hell. The torture of your body being exploited, much against your wishes, has to be experienced to believe. There was no one who could understand my feelings or say a few comforting words.

***

Thereafter I called up and spoke to Karthika when no one was around. We shared our deepest feelings and our sorrow.

She went through more torture than I did. Her husband would get drunk every day and beat her with a belt. Is this hellish life a destiny because we are given the roles of women? Both of us did not like living with men.

But by then, she had two girls.

My mother-in-law insisted that I use the ammi and attukal (stone and pestle) for grinding even though we had a mixie, especially when I was pregnant. She kept me as a slave. My elder sister-in-law and her husband were also staying with us. My mother-in-law would not ask her daughter to do any work. I had to do all the work. I felt like a slave.

I told my amma and called the panchayat and told them that I would survive only if we live independently from his family. The panchayat too supported my decision.

'You have separated me from my son!' my mother-in-law abused and cursed me. I lived in the same locality as my cousin. My husband worked as a piece contractor in a hosiery factory from 8 am–9 pm. I would phone Karthi during this time. She too would call me. We were able to tide over many years like this—ours was a long distance love dependent on the telephone. Because our phone bills were high, our families became suspicious.

My husband called the number that was repeated in the bill and found out that it was Karthika. A huge fight ensued between our families. Each husband accused the other husband that his wife was spoiling the other wife. They cut off the phone connection or kept it locked.

***

Meanwhile, I had a son. For a year, I could not go out of the house. I wondered often about how Karthika was. I could not even talk to her. I wanted to see her in person. One Saturday, I left the baby with my cousin, told my family that I was visiting a temple and went to Karur. It was a one-hour bus ride. Karthika's husband would also return home only at night. Her amma was away in her village.

I called her up when I reached Karur. Her phone was out of order. I guessed that the phone had been cut. But I was bold and went directly to her home. She opened the door. There was no one else at home. We began to cry, trying to say something but failed.

We hugged each other and cried—rage, anger, pain. Our minds and bodies were wounded. Her two girls were away at school. We spoke freely. We even shared with each other stories about how we had sex with our husbands against our desire and even gave birth to children.

Even then, we didn't think that both of us could live together! Because those desires were buried in the sand! Because both of us had children. If two persons seen as women lived together, what would this society say? We never thought of eloping and living together. We wanted to be able to see each other, talk and share our feelings. Because even this was not possible, we suffered a lot.

It was getting late. I had to leave. I had left the baby with my cousin. The man I was forced to marry would return home. We bid a tearful farewell. I took the baby and returned home.

My timing was not right. As soon as I got home, I saw he was there. He was angry that I was not at home.

'Yen di! Where did you go?'

'Went to my cousin's house.'

'Don't lie! Speak the truth! Which man did you go to?'

He hurled abuse at me and made me stand outside the house. He took the baby inside and locked me out. I spent the night outside. After a few hours, he switched on the light and opened the door. He checked if I was there or whether I had left. He then let me in. He did not say a word. At 6 am when I was cooking, he came into the kitchen, 'Where did you go? Which man did you see?' he asked while pulling my hair.

'I did not see any man!' I replied. Heated arguments ensued between us.

He called my parents and elders. 'See how respectable your daughter is!' he mocked them.

'She is not behaving properly. She is talking for hours on the phone with a school friend. Huge bills are being sent every month. Nobody is bothered about husband, child or house. I cannot take this kind of irresponsible behaviour. I wonder which male she goes to visit? Please ask her yourself!' he said.

'Went with some man'—I could not bear those harsh words. Angry, and spurred by my love for Karthi, I declared that I had gone to see her.

He came to hit me with a boulder. The others intervened.

'Go with any man or woman! Leave the son with me!' he said.

'I am the one who gave birth to him. I will go only with him. You get married and have another child!' I retorted.

***

I took my son and walked away.

'What Amma! You did not give us any respect and instead walked out! This is your life. How can you live without a husband? How can you look after your child? Be patient! Let us talk and resolve this!' the elders said to me.

I was not prepared to listen to any one. I decided that I had suffered enough of this hell. I wanted to show people that I could live independently. I boarded the bus to my amma's home.

That was the last time I saw my husband. I lived in my parents' house without my husband after that. Karthika's husband did not know that I had separated from my husband because of her.

My family and society looked upon me with aversion. My cousin stopped talking to me. I began working as a receptionist in a typewriting institute.

Negotiating several challenges, Karthi and I got legally divorced from our respective partners. Today we live with our children in a house together. I dress like a man; but have not undergone surgical change. My son still calls me 'amma.' But he has met many of my trans friends and has begun to understand some things. I hope that one day, my son will grow up, respect my feelings and accept me as the man I am.

Charu left the field of NGO activism, disillusioned with it. He currenlty lives in Bengaluru with Karthi and is setting up a business for self employment.

14

Challenging Life

My parents have six children. Two of them died when they were born. My elder sister is married, my younger brother is in the 12th standard and my younger sister in the 11th. We lived in Warangal, in Andhra Pradesh. We belong to the Lambani tribe.

We live in a Lambani settlement where there are 30 houses. People of other castes also live there. My father was a labourer who earned ₹25 every day. Only my younger brother and older sister went to school. I did not—I was a girl, and was physically handicapped— I've had polio since I was five.

One day, a teacher from our village scolded my parents for not sending me to school and forced them to enrol me. The school was two kilomteres from our house. The teacher took me on his motorbike and that was how I joined Class 1. If that teacher had not supported me, I would not have gone to school. I was nine then. If he had not taken me to school, no one at home would have done so. My classmates regarded me as an oddity because I was physically challenged.

The teacher taught me well from Class 1–3. Because I did well, I was promoted from Class 3 directly to Class 7. Despite being a physically challenged Lambani child seen as a girl, I studied up to the final year degree.

When I was born my legs were normal and healthy. I suddenly contracted polio when I was three or four years old. My left leg was affected first. My parents spent a lot of money on the treatment. Initially I walked on all fours. Then, I was able to walk in a sitting position. Later, even my right leg became bent and weak. By the time I was five years old, I had lost the use of both my legs.

I always sat by myself on the last bench in class. No one would talk to me and everyone avoided me. I felt sad that I could not play with other children. Nobody even bothered to ask me to join them in games. I would sit under a tree and watch them play. I would be dressed like a boy in shorts and shirt. It was convenient for me. Fortunately for me, no one compelled me to dress like a girl. I wore my younger brother's clothes and even cut my hair short like my brother. No one objected to this. When I was in Class 7, my teacher got me a bicycle with three wheels for handicapped people.

In Class 7, I began to feel more strongly that I was a boy, although physiologically I was a girl. During my school examinations, a medical camp was conducted in Tirupati where the government offered surgery free of cost for people affected by polio. I missed my Class 7 exams and went for the camp. At the camp, I saw many people like me. For three days, my parents, uncle and I lived on the hospital footpath, hoping to be called to be examined by the doctors. The camp officials told us that we had to wait for our turn, as there was a long list of people before us. After the doctor examined me he said that I required five operations on my affected leg. And even after that they cautioned us that there was no guarantee of a cure. My parents were frightened. They reasoned that as I was, there was limited mobility at least. What if I developed other complications after surgery? Unwilling to take the risk, they took me back home.

***

I lost a year of school because I had missed the annual examination. I was 15 years old when I completed Class 7. On account of my age, the school authorities sent me to Class 9. I got my periods when I was in Class 7. I was shocked to see the blood that first time. Why did I bleed from that place? The teacher reassured me that it was nothing to worry about and asked my elder sister to take me home. At that time I did not know that this was natural for girls. My friends and family told me, 'You've become a big girl!' I detested the monthly torture. I was troubled by menstruation and felt there was nothing to celebrate.

The Lambani community has an elaborate coming of age ceremony for girls when they get their first period. I had seen it done for my elder sister. However I was certain that I did not want to dress up in a paavaadai dhavani (a half sari over a full skirt) and blouse, with flowers on my head and sit on a wooden pallet. I created a ruckus, cried and threw tantrums and successfully prevented the ceremony from taking place.

Even at that young age, I would cut my hair even shorter than men. I would dress in my younger brother's trousers when he took them off to be washed. In our community, women had to pierce their ears and nose. The family forcefully pierced my ears. But I removed my earrings the very next day.

At school, going to the bathroom was a huge challenge for me. While the class was on, I sneaked out and used the boys' toilet. I don't know why I preferred this to the girl's toilet.

When I was in Class 9, a girl named Sravanthi, who was also physically challenged, joined my class. But she was dressed like a girl in a skirt and blouse and her hair was braided. At first she thought I was a boy. Gradually she came to know that I was a girl who looked like a boy. We became good friends. Sravanthi's younger sister Radhika was in Class 7 in another school.

In Class 10, Sravanthi switched to wearing salwar kameez. My teacher said I should do so as well. I was not used to this because I had never worn women's clothes. I began to hide my developing breasts with books. While having a bath, rather than my polio-affected legs, I was more disturbed at my breasts.

When I was in 11th standard, Sravanthi invited me to her house. I went there along with her. She asked me sit and went inside to change. There I saw Radhika for the first time. She thought I was her elder sister's friend. Radhika offered me tea. All along she had thought that I was a boy; but now she realized that I was not the kind of boy she thought I was. I began to have lunch at Sravanthi's place because it was near the college where I was. Radhika would see me often but not talk to me. But sometimes, she would taunt me and say, 'You are a boy! I will marry you!' Even Sravanthi parents joked, 'If you were a boy we would have accepted you as our son-in-law!'

Suddenly one day Radhika gave me a letter. She said, 'Go home and read it when no one is around.'

She wrote in the letter, 'Kiran, I love you. I want to marry you. If I don't see you for a day, I am unable to sleep. I want you to always be with me in my house.'

***

I did not know if she was serious or playing a joke on me. I took a week to think about this. Next week I went to her home and said to her, 'I need to talk to you alone. Please come to the college ground.'

'Don't joke with me. I have many issues at home. Let us not spoil the relationships we have.' I sent her home with this advice.

Two months later, Radhika showed me a newspaper clipping of two women who were married.

'Why can't we two get married like this?' she asked.

'Are you mad? Is it so easy for the two of us to get married? Will society accept such a marriage?' I argued with her. 'Radhika! Let's treat this as a joke. Sravanthi and I have a good friendship and I don't wish to spoil it.'

But she was not prepared to listen.

'Do you love me or not?' she asked petulantly. She was like a child who could not take 'No' for an answer. 'Will you marry me?'

I did not know what to say. 'Give me some time.' I stammered and I left the place.

***

I spent the whole night thinking about this incident. I was attracted to girls. I also made fun of other girls about being with me. I did not know if the girl I loved would be with me forever. But today, more than me loving a girl, the fact that a girl loved me, was something special. I was sure that she would be with me forever.

On Radhika's birthday, I bought her a sari and went to her place. This was my way of expressing my love for her. However, on her birthday, Radhika suddenly developed acute stomach pain and had to be admitted to hospital. She needed to have her appendix removed. She refused treatment and insisted on seeing me. Her parents telephoned me and I went to the hospital. The doctor was shocked because she said that she would get treated only if she saw me. When she saw me she was delighted and agreed to get treated.

By then, I realized that Radhika truly loved me and I felt I must reciprocate her love. I was in Class 12 and she was in Class 10. We celebrated her birthday the day after she was discharged from the hospital. It was a cold day in December. I spent the night with her alone in a room. Our love, which, until now, was at the level of feelings, now expressed itself freely through our bodies. We became really close to one another—emotionally and physically.

A few months later I developed a blood clot in my stomach and fainted. I underwent surgery. Both our families visited me and they became friendly with each other after that. Radhika started visiting me and also cooking for me at home when I was recovering.

I then joined a Mahila Sanghathan (women's organization) and my job was to record the minutes of the meetings. I was paid a monthly salary of ₹2000. In the meantime, Vimala told me that her family was trying to fix a matrimonial alliance for Radhika. I was deeply saddened and shocked when I heard this. How could I tell Sravanthi that I was in love with Radhika?

Radhika knew that the bridegroom's family was coming to see her. She called me and told me everything.

'I am not interested in this marriage. I want you.'

She was firm in her resolve.

'Tell me, what can I do now?' I asked in despair.

'Take me away. Or I will commit suicide', she threatened.

Within a year of her engagement, on Sivarathri, both of us went to the beach. She once again showed me the newspaper clipping of a lesbian couple who had married in Karimnagar.

'Let's get married there.'

***

I was apprehensive. But love overruled logic and reason. We decided to go to Tirupati. I had seen an advertisement for free marriages in Tirupati. Once there, I told them that I was physically challenged, and that her family opposed the marriage. I did not reveal my gender. They said they would get us married. We then returned to our homes. I told my family that there was an office tour to Tirupati and got their permission to go. My mother sent my 13-year-old cousin along with me. I had no other choice but to accept this. I stole ₹2000, which my father had saved and went to Radhika's house.

Radhika asked me if she should bring something from her house.

'Nothing. I have money with me. Just take the sari I gave you', I said.

Radhika was wearing a ring and the sari I had given her. She left behind a 20-page letter to her parents that she had written. I was not aware of it then.

We boarded the train. My innocent cousin knew nothing about our love. Radhika and I were frightened and tense. I switched off my mobile. It was 13 hours from Warangal to Tirupati. We reached Tirupati at night.

I tonsured my head and went to the wedding hall where wedding ceremonies were performed free of charge. I had photocopies of my ration card and voter ID, in which I had changed my name to Kiran instead of Usha. It also stated that although I was physiologically a female, I now lived like a male. I told the authorities that I was physically challenged and that our families opposed the marriage. I was 23 years old, and Radhika was 21.

Radhika and I got married. Funnily, my 13-year-old cousin was the only witness to our marriage!

Until I tied the wedding knot on Radhika's neck, I was nervous. What if someone from my home saw us? After that, Radhika mustered the courage to make the first call to her family. Only then did I realize that Radhika's family had gone to my place in search of her. Since I was not there they had filed a police complaint that Usha (as I was known to family and friends) had kidnapped Radhika! They had beaten up my father and fought with him. He had to be hospitalised. My mother, in a fit of despair, had drunk poison.

After both of us had phoned our families and told them we were married, switched off our mobiles. We left for my elder sister's home at Nizamabad and we sent my cousin home. My elder sister accepted us smilingly and welcomed us with the traditional welcome accorded for a newly married couple. It was ironical that while we were receiving a warm welcome, there was a terrible storm brewing in our respective homes in Warangal. The next day the news of our wedding was splashed in the local media—two women got married! My sister was now worried and scared about the impact of this publicity on our lives and hers.

My sister now said to us, 'Surrender to the police. This has become a serious issue.' As she was talking to us, media persons from TV news channels had also arrived. My sister insisted that neither Radhika nor I should talk to them. However, Radika insisted that we talk. She felt that our story needed to be told to the media because she feared that her family would take her home and get her forcibly married to another man. I admired Radhika's courage and presence of mind. Certainly, in both these qualities, she was better than me.

***

Radhika talked to the media. We then surrendered to the local district police station. Her family thought that I had kidnapped Radhika to get her married to someone else. They could not in their wildest imagination believe that instead *I* had married *her*! Not me! They did not even believe my cousin who was witness to our wedding! Even the police was confused!

Here is a part of Radhika's live interview on TV.

Media: 'By choosing to marry a woman, you have married against the laws of nature. How will society view this marriage? Who will support you? How will you lead a life? What about having kids?'

Radhika, 'We are even prepared to beg to survive! We can adopt if we want kids.'

Radhika's courage and determination gave me all the strength I needed. She was an inspiration for me.

She led by example. My only fear was that at the district level I was well known as a disability rights activist. I feared public disapproval due to my unconventional marriage.

However, we were disturbed and angry when the media asked us insensitive questions like 'how will you have sex?' At Warangal, the public, enraged by what they perceived as 'unnatural' behaviour, flung slippers at us.

I was overwhelmed in the face of all this hate. Radhika was my pillar of support and strength. Meanwhile, Sangama staff contacted an NGO office at Hyderabad which became our sanctuary; our place of refuge. We learnt that they worked for the rights of people like us. In the midst of all this media madness, there was a ray of sunshine too. Gemini TV was supportive of our case. They did a programme on the human rights violations we had experienced in this journey.

The NGO requested the hijra community to help us. They all came forward to support us. We were seeing hijras for the first time. We were scared at that time. We were in Hyderabad for one week. When we interacted with hijras, we realized that our fears were completely due to the negative stereotypes about them. They took care of us and protected us.

We then shifted to Bengaluru and were provided shelter for two years by another branch of the NGO.

I had worked in the field of disability activism and human rights for many years. But after my marriage to Radhika, no one supported me. The popular opinion among people was that we should not be allowed to enter Warangal. They wanted us to just die somewhere! I hope that stories of people like us will help raise more awareness about others like us and enable more people to come out in support for us. I continue my work as a trans man in the field of gender and disability rights in the hope of making some change. And Radhika's devoted presence by my side through all these years still gives me strength and hope to carry on. Instead of being challenged, over time, I have found the strength to challenge life.

Kiran is a trans and disability rights activist. He currently lives in Chickballapur in Karnataka with his wife Radhika.

15

Boys to Men

When my patti (grandmother) died, my mother and her sister were still small children. Patti had written off her agricultural fields to her brother, as her children were too young. She told him at the time that the land had to be equally divided between the girls when they got married.

My chitti (mother's younger sister) got married. Although my mother was pregnant with me, she was not married. I do not know who my father was or even his name.

My mama (maternal uncle) uncle gave a share of the property only to chitti. When amma (mother) asked for her share, uncle said, 'Bring your husband! Show him to me! You are a good for nothing sucker!' and drove her out.

Amma worked as a domestic help in several houses. A few days after I was born, she handed me over to a nurse and asked her to bring me up. I did not even see my mother's face in those days. I grew up in the nurse's house. As I grew older, I yearned to see my mother.

Some people told me that amma was a sex worker. At that age I did not know what that meant.

***

My mother was in regular contact with the nurse during that period. One day, however, amma returned. She took me to chitti's house and stayed with me. Because she was a sex worker, chitti gave her separate plate, drinking glass and bed. But they didn't hesitate to take her money!

That was how I was with Amma for some time. In Class 9, however, I was in a relative's house. I hated my mother till class 8 because she was not around. Then, one day when we were staying together, I read her diary. I felt terrible. She had written about her struggle to raise me and how even her child didn't understand her.

When I was in 12th standard, amma died. She was 40 years old. She had a high blood pressure condition, diabetes, kidney problems and a heart problem. Chitti had no children. She took up a job in Saudi Arabia as a cook in a house. So I had to cook for chittappa (uncle, my chitti's husband). But his behaviour disturbed me. He tried to force me to sleep with him and threatened me that if I did not, he would not give me my share of the ancestral property. I wrote to my chitti and told her about this. But I got no reply. I knew that she did not believe me.

During those days, I wore a shirt over a skirt. I buttoned it up like a man. I wanted to cut my hair short like men do. After Class 10, I cut my hair. Sundaram, someone who was like me and who studied with me, sported a short cropped hair cut. I cut my hair because I was inspired by him! Fortunately for me, there were no rules in college that girls should not cut their hair like boys. But people would always order me to behave like a girl and not a boy. I also looked like the other boys!

Sundaram and I were called Shikhandi and made fun of—because people felt that both of us were neither girl nor boy. Sundaram and I would tease girls like other boys. But although we wanted to, we did not flirt with the girls. We were too scared of getting into trouble. We just passed comments about them.

Chittappa did not like my haircut and the fact that I dressed in trousers and shirts. My neighbours often advised me, 'Be like a family woman. We are poor. And therefore have to behave like decent women.'

'I am a cricket player. So I have to dress like this because it's comfortable,' I lied to them. My chittappa forced me to wear churidhars instead of pants and shirt. I could not stand his torture. One day I shouted at him, 'Are people like you fathers?'

Furious at me for confronting him, he hit me on the thighs with a rod. My thighs became black and blue with bruises. I immediately told my neighbours and showed them what he had done. They asked me to tell my chitti. Although I wrote to her, she did not reply. I told my neighbours that she was not replying to my letters. I then sent her photos of my injured thighs. She said she would talk to him. But she didn't believe that he made passes at me. I felt guilty because I thought that I was being punished for something I had done wrong. Meanwhile, I knew Sasi who was a distant relative. He taught me how to write love letters. Sasi worked in a driving school. He is one of my oldest trans friends. Much before any of us had begun living as socially male, he had bravely ventured into that world.

Sundaram and I often visited Sasi. His mother had a small shop. She often said, 'Too bad he is like this. Even his friends are like him!'

Sasi once said to me, 'If we want to become men, our lips must become black. Let's smoke a lot of beedis!' He stole beedis from his mother and we smoked together.

While I was in my 12th, I did not write my exams because in the women's college I was dressing like a man. The parents of the other students complained about me. Hence I quit college and roamed around with Sasi and Sundaram. I was jealous of them because they looked like boys. They bound their chest tightly and wore banians and shirts.

Sasi said, 'If you wet appalam (papad) and bind it tight on the chest, the breasts will shrivel and shrink.' Desperate, I followed Sasi's advice faithfully and hoped for the miracle of shrivelled and shrunk breasts. Unfortunately they did not shrink! Worse, they only became bigger! If we wanted a moustache, we drew it with coal from the fire.

***

Through Sasi I heard about an organization in Kerala that works with trans people like us. The organization invited us to the World Social Forum (WSF) in Mumbai. I found the culture in Kerala, with its patriarchal stereotypes to be very restrictive. The WSF was a perfect opportunity for me to escape from my troublesome uncle. I told him that I was going for a cricket match and instead went to Mumbai.

I discovered that Mumbai had some liberating spaces. At WSF I met differently gendered people like me and lesbians and gays. I was able to express myself freely there—be myself; be a man. For the first time, I felt that my feelings regarding my gender identity were validated by others. The WSF was a turning point in my life. I met Famila there for the first time. She was very attractive.

Christy knew Famila earlier. He said to her, 'He (Sonu) wants to have sex with you. He will give you ₹100.'

Famila replied, 'I will not come for ₹100. I charge ₹500.'

I said to her, 'I have only ₹100. Interested?'

We laughed till our sides split. In my place, a man and a woman could not talk so freely like this. For the first time, I felt happy. Only as I talked to Famila did I realize she was a trans woman and a part of the hijra community. She had undergone surgery to make herself into the woman I saw before my eyes.

I was born female but wished to live like a male. Could I also get operated? When I came to know that Famila was a hijra, I was frightened. I had heard a lot of negative things about the hijra community. It is only when you move closely with the community that you really get to know them. I soon got rid of all my prejudices. But we still have not been able to do that in the larger society, which remains prejudiced about trans people in general, and hijras in particular.

Famila's loving and affectionate nature touched me. Famila was a black beauty. Although I had been attracted to several girls, nobody could match Famila. I saw Famila as a woman and not as a hijra. She regarded me as a man and called me 'vaa da, poda.' (Masculine pronouns in Tamil). At the WSF sessions, all of us ate together. We participated in the various events there.

It was there that I heard Revathi amma's speech for the first time. Revathi amma was Famila's guru. Until then I did not know that there were hijras who talked so eloquently like her. Famila's face lit up with joy when she heard her 'Mummy' speak. She clapped the loudest for her.

After the WSF, for one week I stayed in Bengaluru before going home to Thiruvananthapuram, the capital of Kerala. My family and neighbours disliked me roaming around because I was seen as a woman. They pressurized me to get married. But I desired to live as a man. Only after WSF did I begin to believe that I too could live like a man. This was because I met many others like me.

I ran away from home and went to Bengaluru, to Famila's house. Famila worked as a sex worker. Famila's home was a sanctuary for many trans men like me, and for trans women and lesbians. She provided all of us a safe space with food, shelter and security. She was a generous soul whose heart reached out to those in distress. I was deeply touched by her compassion and was filled with immense love, affection and respect for her. I too needed the love that she showered on people like us. We decided to live together. She shared the good and bad experiences of sex work with me. Gradually I too realized the struggles and pain she had experienced to transition to womanhood.

Ironically those organs in the body Famila did not want were the ones I wanted and vice versa. I wanted to get a sex change operation done but when I heard the pain she underwent following it, I was scared. Famila told me that even if I don't get operated, she would still see me as a man. I knew that reconstructing a penis (phalloplasty) was a difficult surgery but at least

I wanted to get rid of my breasts (mastectomy). She even took me to a doctor who did breast removal surgery. Even then, I was scared. I was highly anxious and a thousand unanswered questions troubled me. How will the doctor remove the breasts? Will it hurt? Will it look attractive? Will it cause other problems?

Although Famila and I were lovers, we did not behave like lovers in a male dominated society. Although I identified as a man, I did not believe in control and that all power rests only with men. We did not follow strict gender roles in our relationship. We shared all work. She introduced me as 'my partner' to others and I loved that.

Revathi Mummy approved of our relationship. She often playfully asked me, '*Enna da marumagane* (Hello, son-in-law), how are you?' But there were others in the hijra community who did not approve. Although they had changed themselves into women, they found it difficult to accept that we wanted to change ourselves into men. They were critical of Famila's relationship with me. They also abused Revathi amma for having a troublesome and disobedient chela like Famila.

Famila was furious with them. She demanded, 'We can change into women, so they can change into men. Why can't they?' Famila and I wanted to spearhead a social revolution of sorts. We wanted to legally get married to each other. We wanted ID proofs like voter IDs, ration cards. Famila too could not get an ID as a woman. But some members of the hijra community had voter ID cards saying that they were women. They undergo surgery, grow their hair, wear saris, pierce their ears and nose and pass off as women. But what about us? Unless we too undergo surgery and take hormones to grow a beard and moustache, how can we bravely say that we are men?

Famila was a treasure. I was blessed to have had her in my life. Many friends shared Famila's home. Our happiness, however, was short-lived. She shared her joys and sorrows, but did not fully divulge what was in her mind. Even today nobody knows why she committed suicide. Her death is a loss to the female to male transgender community—she was our biggest spokesperson. After her death, all of us went our separate ways. Famila was my only solace and strength. After her death, I joined an NGO and started working for LGBT activism.

***

Female to male trans people like me have no family support. There is absolutely no awareness in society about people like us. Very few organizations support us and give us work. Even among the hijra community, only some people support us. Unlike male to female trans persons, we lack community support structures such as the hijra jamaat, the guru-chela bonding, living together etc. NGOs also mostly focus on HIV work.

I could get a voter ID/passport, PAN card and bank account in my given name. I detest being referred to or addressed by my female name. Although at the work place legally I have my female name, my colleagues referred to me as 'Sonu'. I give more respect and regard for my feelings rather than my body. I hate my breasts. I have waited all my life to remove them.

I often ask my friends, 'Shall I chop them off myself?' Not that I need their permission to do so. But this just emphasizes how much I experience the need to remove all traces of my female anatomy because that was never part of who I am. My clothes, hairstyle, perfume/deodorant, watch, and footwear—are all men's fashion. I used to shave my face regularly because they said that this would cause facial hair to grow quickly.

While hijras take hormones to make their skin soft, with female to male trans persons it is the opposite. However, in both communities, nobody follows systems and procedures. Most of us look for quick fixes and immediate results. For instance, a person wishing to undergo sex change has to follow a systematic and often long process that involves consultations with psychiatrists, counsellors, endocrinologists and surgeons. It is illegal to do so otherwise. But only a small percentage follows this recommended protocol. Sadly doctors also do not know much about us and do not treat us sensitively. Some doctors also delay the process endlessly making us more desperate.

I once developed an abscess in the genital area. I did not consult a doctor, as I believed it was due to body heat. My friends advised me to see a doctor, as they were certain that it would get infected. I felt ashamed to go to one. Because although I had a female body, I dressed like a man. What will doctors ask me when they look at the way I am dressed? Meanwhile, the abscess became big and I was unable to walk.

One of my community members took me to a doctor who understood us. 'I know about your community. Don't worry. Let me examine you,' he reassured me.

But we feel embarrassed to show our breasts or genitals. Some doctors, when they see us, start to interrogate us. This is more important to them than the treatment they have to offer. This hurts us. But we also understand that there is a female name on the case sheet but we behave and dress like men. So while I suppose it is natural for them to cross question us, it is difficult and painful for us. We do wish that doctors were more sensitive and informed about our special needs and concerns as female to male trans persons

Despite being told that the doctor was aware of the issues faced by female to male trans persons, when he saw me, he asked, 'Are you male or female?' I joked, 'That's what I am here to find out!' I decided not to get treated by him.

***

After I came to Bengaluru, I began to live as a man. I often go with trans men to bars. I love that freedom! I want to smoke and drink freely and have lots of fun! But when I go to bars, using the toilet is a problem. We wish to use male toilets but are unable to stand and pee. Besides these toilets have no doors. So what do we do?

Once Revathi amma and I went to Chennai on official work. At the Koyambedu bus stand we had to use the toilet. I was wondering what to do. The male toilet had no doors. Using the women's toilet was humiliating as a man. But I had no choice. As I was stepping out, a 55-year-old man, a security guard at the bus stand caught me by the collar. 'Which bathroom are you going into?' he shouted at me. I did not know what to tell him.

Revathi amma said to him, 'Leave him! A woman will go into woman's bathroom.' He looked at me up and down. My breasts told him I am a woman. And he let me go.

Hjras are referred to as 'aval' (a feminine pronoun in Tamil)). Female to male trans persons are referred to as 'avan' (the masculine pronoun in Tamil). Some people call us 'adiye' (another form of feminine pronoun in Tamil). If they did so out of ignorance, it's fine. But if they do it knowingly, we get hurt. Some hijras mockingly refer to us as 'sapti bhaji' or lesbians, which we are not. We are heterosexuals. Hijras, are born male and change into the female gender. They are puzzled at my rejection of my female identity.

They often tell me, 'God has given you all this. Why do you say you don't want this body?'

Because we are born female and wish to live as male, we don't like to have breasts or a vagina. In meetings where trans men, women, kothis, gays and lesbians are present, some hijras make obscene gestures such as rubbing their hands together and with a sly smirk refer to us as 'sapti bhaji!' This annoys us—we keep telling them we are not like that, that we are also heterosexual men with women partners, but often people do not listen.

However, there *are* people in the hijra community who understand us. People like Revathi amma and Famila. People like them support us unconditionally. They give us comfort and tell us, 'Don't worry! We understand your feelings!'

Slowly, more trans women, through years of work, are beginning to understand and accept us. I hope that our stories will also help create more awareness about us.

I started hormone replacement therapy two years back and also underwent surgery. Now, several issues

I have mentioned in my early life have disappeared. I do not get stared at on the roads anymore. I have a thick beard and moustache and I am finally the man I always wanted to be. Many other female to male trans persons are still struggling like I was earlier, and I hope that our work will help make life easier for them in future.

Sonu Niranjan is a trans activist and singer. He recently acted in a documentary on his life called That's My Boy *directed by Akhil Sathyan. He lives in Bengaluru.*

16

Birth of a Man

Among Christians, when a person dies, there is a particular ritual that is performed only by men. My mother too was there, participating on one such occasion. I wondered why Mummy was there as only men were supposed to do this ritual. I was puzzled. I even asked my periamma (mother's elder sister), about this.

She said, 'She is two in one!'

I wondered what she meant. I'd read about Shikhandi in the *Mahabharata*, and heard of names like ombodu, ponduga, napumsakar, khoja (all derogatory references in Tamil to physiological males who identified themselves as female). Was my mother also someone like them?

When I asked periamma she said to me frankly, 'Your mother was born male, but changed into female and then went to Mumbai and often visits Bengaluru.'

Periamma told me that I was adopted. My mother adopted me in in Mumbai, along with two other girls. Their names were Sunita and Anita. My family used to lovingly call me pet names like Sivapi and Kempamma because I was fair. Amma lived in Mumbai and would occasionally visit us in Bengaluru. Periamma looked after me. My sisters were brought up by another periamma. Amma's younger brother was a rowdy of sorts. He often fought with her for no reason. But she was the one who got him married. She also sent him to Dubai.

I don't know if periamma had a husband. Apparently he died before I came into the family. Her children were married and well settled. She lived with us because she had decided to look after me. When I was ten years old, I desired to look at my mother's body. How would she look? How would it be for her down there, between her legs? From where would I have been born?

When amma wanted her back scrubbed, she always asked for me because she liked the way I gave her a hard, soothing scrub. Under the pretext of scrubbing her back, I would try to take a peek at her private parts. What a disappointment! I could only see her big tummy and thighs! During festivals, we would visit my grandparents' graves and offer prayers. Property disputes then arose between amma and her brother. The extended family believed that if the property were in her name, it would be passed on to us 'orphans'.

***

We lived in amma's brother's home, which we partitioned into two. Amma drank, smoked bidis and also used pan parag—all in front of us. When she ran out of bidi or parag, she would ask me to get her new stock. At school, I would stylishly hold a cigarette and pretend to smoke like man! I would stealthily steal a cigarette or two and go to the terrace and experiment with smoking.

At first, we lived with amma's elder brother. He had five children. I never liked them. Three of them sexually harassed me. Even before I had come of age. Despite calling them 'anna' (elder brother) they would touch me rather oddly in places where they should not. Amma hardly spent time with me, even when she visited me from Mumbai. So I could never tell her about my cousins. But she would get me all sorts of things that I wanted and more even if I did not ask her.

One of the cousins was openly sexually suggestive. He would insert his hands in his pockets, shake his dick and make sure that I noticed it. I felt sacred even to look at him. He would get me ice creams and make me sleep next to him. At other times, he would beat me.

Today when I look back at his behaviour, I feel he breached the trust I had in him. I feel like abusing him verbally and spitting on his face. I once told amma about this. I was not sure if she even registered what I was trying to tell her. Once he did the same thing to my older sister and then it became a big fight. Only after this incident, did we move into the Dubai brother's home.

I attended church on Sundays but would leave during Mass. I disliked sitting inside the church, praying, singing. But I loved playing the drums. Had they given that to me, I would have sat eternally inside the church! When the girls came out after Mass, I would 'gaze' at them and stand outside the compound so that I could do that endlessly.

Our school uniform was a blue skirt, blue tie and white shirt. We had to tuck in our shirts. I would tuck it in on one side and leave the other side loose and even lift my collar up like a rowdy! My science teacher would twist my ears and ask me to dress 'properly'. I wanted to dress like men. But this was the nearest I could get to satisfying those desires. Every day I got into trouble with the same teacher because she felt I was not dressing like a girl.

But at home I behaved innocently because my mother was strict. So I tried all this only outside the home. Otherwise I did everything that men usually do—operating the music system, dancing to Telugu film music, arranging tables and chains and changing bulbs. I even helped with construction work in our house—by watering the ceiling and even carried pots of water in both my hands or on my shoulders.

Amma frowned when she saw me lift pots of water this way.

'Girls don't do it this way! Learn to lift the pot on your hips like a good girls!" she scolded me. I tried to do so but only ended up breaking the pots! Not ready to give up, amma filled a big pot of water, placed it on my hips and stood next to me with a big stick.

'Now let me see how it will fall!' she threatened. The pot was slipping away but I supported it with my hands because I was afraid she would beat me. Amma was involved in social service. She spearheaded agitations for water taps in the village, obtained schoolbooks for those children who needed them and presided over Kannada Rajyostava functions. As I accompanied her on several such occasions, many people also knew me.

***

When I was in Class 9, I had a friend Bhagya, who was in Class 10. My elder sister was married in the same town as Bhagya. Bhagya and I were friendly with each other. I fell in love with her. She was a good dancer and a high-ranking student. We were together in a group dance in school. I did not want to dance like a girl but I decided to do so because at least I could dance with Bhagya! But I realized at the new school opening function, that we all had to simply dress like animals. I was so relieved by this!

In our school, the classrooms of Classes 8, 9 and 10 were in a straight line. I was good at studies till Class 7. But after that, my marks dropped, particularly in Maths. I behaved like a rowdy. My behaviour was typical of what would be considered masculine. I often made fun of the girls. The teachers often made me stand outside the class because of my poor performance and my unruly behaviour.

While I stood out, I could see at Bhagya who was in the classroom parallel to mine. So I would do all sorts of antics to be punished and sent out. I once wrote her a letter and even proposed to her! She laughed at me. She thought I was being comical.

I told Bhagya that I was in love with her. She in turn told her friends that I was in love with her! They all laughed heartily. Bhagya handed over my letter to Anthony Mary, a teacher and a friend of my mother's!

The teacher demanded that I see her and launched an enquiry.

"What's this? What do you think you are doing?" she demanded angrily.

It was impossible for me to hide my feelings for Bhagya.

'I love her!' I retorted sharply.

The teacher thought that I was an aggressive girl who behaved like an unruly boy to make life tough for her. However, she thought that the reason I behaved aggressively was because my mother was a trans woman! She warned me to control my behaviour.

I hardly listened to what she had to say. I followed Bhagya around. On the pretext of visiting my sister, I would try to see Bhagya. I waited for her in school compound. All this irritated Bhagya. She began to avoid me and sat in the last row so I could not see her. Even then, I did not give up. I craned my neck to see her. I would be over enthusiastic to run errands for my teachers like getting a chalk piece, because these tasks allowed me to catch some glimpses of Bhagya!

During the interval I would get her chocolates, greeting cards and flowers. She would throw away the chocolates, tear the greeting cards and crush the flowers. Once she said to me, 'Aren't you ashamed? You are a girl and you give a love letter to another girl!'

***

In one of the answer papers in the half yearly exam I had scrawled, 'I am sorry, Bhagya' all over the answer sheet! The teacher who was supervising caught me during the exam and took me to the principal. I was asked,'What's happening between the two of you!'

Bhagya disclosed all that had happened so far, She ended with, 'Like her mother, she is also two-in-one!'

I was not hurt that Bhagya had insulted me. But what made me both angry and sad was that she had insulted my mother. Enraged, I hit her on the head with the duster and broke her head.

I admit that I should not have done that. But I was furious that she had dragged my mother into all this. The matter became serious. They called my periamma to school. My home was just five minutes away from the school. I was suspended for six months. I got a letter saying I was being suspended for having some mental problems. I lost one year of school because of this.

My periamma thrashed me in public till I reached home. Everyone looked at me like I had done something with some boy. I was very insulted.

When I went home from school my mother was frying fish in a big wok. She asked me to sit next to her. I was scared. Would she pour the hot oil on to me?

She cried and asked, 'Why are you behaving this way? What have I done wrong? Being a hjira, I brought you up with good values. Now, people will say, "The child the hijra she has brought up will only be like her!"'

I was silent. My mother beat me on my head and it broke into two halves. I was bleeding profusely. But I was stoic. I soon became unconscious and was taken to hospital where my head was sutured.

During that time, I was given a separate plate and separate food at home. They did not let me mingle with others. They spoke to me indirectly without addressing me, like they were speaking to the wall. All old food or the leftovers were given to me. Even after my sister had a baby, they wouldn't let me touch it because they thought the baby would become like me. They forced me to wear only half saree, not even churidar. They tried to exorcise the spirit in me through exorcists in Hindu, Muslim, Christian faiths. Some people also said that I would be cured if I were married off.

As I was short tempered and impulsive by nature, my mother kept quiet for a few days. Later she told me to quit school. She took me to Mumbai with her and

I had to cook at home. I was not happy about the move. My mother was strict with me. She would beat me if I overcooked or undercooked food. She beat me with the lid of the cooker whenever she food my cooking unsatisfactory. To save me form my mother's violence, the hijra akka (elder sister) who shared the home with us, offered to cook secretly. But my mother found this out and insisted that only I should cook. She also sternly instructed the akka not to protect me. I now led a constrained life. Just like a woman. I detested doing all the domestic chores that they forced me to do.

***

I returned to Bengaluru with my mother's younger brother. Once there, I became my usual self—behaving boisterously, laughing loudly and dancing without any inhibitions. My periamma told my mother about what she considered inappropriate behaviour for a girl. My mother then decided to get me married to a man in Mumbai. I became even more scared now, because I knew my mother would ensure that it happened soon. My problem was that I wanted to marry a woman and that too only Bhagya!

The only option for me was to run away form home. It was Christmas evening and everyone at home was absorbed in making rangoli. I packed my clothes (men's clothes) and monkey cap. I wore a kameez and churidhar over my shirt. I stole ₹5000 from the tenant. My family members were at church attending the midnight mass. Fortunately, I had the presence of mind to tell my family about my unwillingness to go to church on the pretext that I was unwell.

A LIFE IN TRANS ACTIVISM

Although periamma had locked the gate, I climbed over the it and escaped. I ran across fields and bushes in search of the main road.

I had covered everything except for my face. A man on a cycle came and followed me, asking me for the time. I didn't tell him the time because I was scared he would catch onto my gender by my voice. He took me to the fields and tried to rape me. I cried out loud. Some workers at a brick kiln nearby came running and rescued me. They had a shed near the brick kiln. I stayed there in the shed that night.

It was 7 a.m. when I left that place and reached the main road. I wore full pants and tucked my kameez in. I had taken care to wear a full-sleeved kameez to cover my bangles. I wore a monkey cap to hide my hair. I saw a mechanic's workshop in that deserted place. Fortunately, it was open. I asked the mechanic for directions to the Shivaji Nagar church.

There was no direct bus and so I had to take two buses before to reach the bus stop. I waited at the bus stop the whole day. I had ₹5000, a gold chain and a ring with me. I met two footpath cloth dealers and begged them for a job. When they asked me about my earlier work experience, I told him that I had worked in garments before.

They took me to their place and said that they would get me a job tomorrow. Perhaps they guessed I was a girl. They took me to a deserted building under construction. I sensed they were planning to assault me. One of them touched me in a strange way. He stroked my bum. I said to him, 'I don't like all this! Take your hands off!'

Another man put his arm causally round me and stroked my breast, as if accidentally. I pushed him away and tried to escape. They pulled my bag and prevented me from escaping. I left my bag behind and ran away. I reached Shivaji Nagar bus stand and spent the night there. I did not know where to go. Did I make a mistake in running away?

***

I decided to chop off my hair. At least this would make me less recognizable as a woman. When I went to the barber shop, he was surprised that I wanted to chop off such long hair.

I ordered the surprised barber, 'Chop it off! You need only the money, right?'

I got myself men's shoes, a watch and bracelet and once again went towards the bus stand. Meanwhile, someone employed at the bus stop had noticed that I'd been loitering there for two days. He spoke to me. I was not sacred of him, as he seemed a respectable man. He was a government bus mechanic. I frankly told him about my desire to live like a man and the problems it had caused in my family.

'I want to change into a man. My family is opposed to this idea and wanted to get me married to man. So I've run away from home, Uncle.'

He took me home. I met his wife and kids. His wife suspected that I was a runaway.. 'How can you run away? You are a 17-year-old girl. I will telephone your mother.'

'She'll force me to get married. If you don't like me being here, I'll go away,' I reasoned with her.

She phoned her husband and said to him, 'The girl wants to go away.'

I left their home and went towards a tea stall near the footpath. There was a hotel close by. I was standing in front of a bar near the hotel. A speeding car stopped near me. I noticed a man inside the car. He had a beer bottle in his hand and was staring at me. I pretended not to notice him.

He called me after a while. I boldly sat in the car.

'I need a job.'

'Drink?'

I wanted to drink. It was my first time. I drank two glasses and was dizzy by the third. He took me to a dark place that was deserted. He tried to rape me. I vomited. He asked me to get down. After I threw up, I felt much better. I refused to get inside the car. Instead I came back to the tea shop in an auto.

The auto driver invited me to his home and introduced me to his wife and children. They were affectionate and loving. I told them the truth about me. But they insisted on reuniting me with my mother. I could not convince them that I did not want to go home to my mother. However, in desperation I said to them.

'Okay, I'll go to my mother's house.'

They seemed satisfied and even felt that they had achieved a big victory. One of the girls even gave me her phone number and said I should get in touch with her if I needed or if there was an emergency. I realized how difficult it was to be safe in a woman's body. I stayed for a day in a church, where the priest was known to my periamma and later moved to a ladies convent for one night. At both places I did not tell them about my gender struggle.

***

The next day at the tea shop I met several people in pants and shirts who looked like me. I met a hijra, Sheetal, who reminded me of my mother. Although I wanted to talk to her, I was scared that she would take me back to my mother.

They took me to the Sangama office at Shivaji Nagar in Bengaluru. I met Revathi amma there for the first time. I was very scared because I did not want to go back home. 'She is also a trans person so she will tell my mother and send me back', I thought. As a staff member of Sangama, she counselled me and said it was not permissible for a minor to stay in the office premises. She contacted my mother and told her that I was there. She then told me that I would not face any trouble at home and sent me back.

When I went back, everyone came to see me like I was some animal in a zoo because I had cut my hair and looked very different. I spoke very strongly that nobody should force me to do anything or I would complain about them. Everyone was taken aback, wondering who would support me. There was a lock on my landline so I that I couldn't call anyone. Nobody would talk to me or eat with me or anything. I knew that they were going to forcefully marry me off. I found the key to the landline from somewhere and called the Sangama office. Someone answered and said everyone has gone to Bombay and asked me to call later. I told the person to book me a ticket to Bombay or I would be married off.

I went to the World Social Forum in Mumbai with people from the office. I met many male to female and female to male trans persons there. But I was very withdrawn and didn't trust anyone because of my recent experiences. Some hijras saw me there and called my mother and she sent her chelas to see me. When they saw the cigarettes in my pocket they teased me and asked me when I became such a big person! They telephoned my mother and asked me to talk with her. But she refused to speak to me.

***

Six years, amma had to be hospitalised. It was then that I went to see her. She was introducing me to another patient as her son but when the other person asked what my name was, my mother didn't know the answer. So at that time, I said, 'Christy'.

She said, 'You have taken care of your life. Be good. You are living as you desire.'

Those were the last words my mother said to me before she died.

Christy Raj is an activist, videographer and dancer. He currently lives in Bengaluru and is an inspiration to many, to live their truths.

17

Emperor Penguins

The wound is the place where the light enters you

—Rumi

As I sat impatiently outside the waiting room to see the doctor who would finally do my top surgery, I took a look around. The doctor's clinic was behind a post office in Borivali West, Bombay. Dr Neeta Patel had a showcase full of honours for plastic surgery. I tried to focus on them to get my mind off a disturbing sight- a picture of Sai Baba that she had garlanded and in front of which rested a lit lamp.

I was accompanied by my mother and Annakutty, my partner at the time. It was a big moment for me. My mother, who had raised me and my brother singlehandedly, was with me as I prepared for a second birth of sorts, in a body closer to what I felt like I should have. When my mother left her marriage and walked out with her two young children, she had a job and some property that was handed down to her from a dominant Shudra caste ancestry.

In hindsight, I wonder if it was the endogamous caste control over my body along with internalised transphobia that made me vacillate between whether or not I should medically transition to become a man. I went back and forth in my head for several years until the choice really became one between life and death. It took me more than two decades of loneliness to find other trans men. This was of course, before the Internet.

When I started living with my brothers, I realised that though a lot of us wanted to transition medically, we had absolutely no idea about surgery, hormones or health care. So, I began a search along with Annakutty, going to all the doctors who I had heard would do the surgery or prescribe hormones. We went to Gujarat, Delhi, Bombay and Tamil Nadu.

Once, during this journey, the general compartment was so full, we decided to travel in the ladies' compartment. I sat on the overhead luggage rack. Soon, men started getting into the compartment and taking over most of the space. A policeman came into the compartment and chased them all away. One man pointed up to me and said, 'What about him?' The policeman grabbed me by the hair and dragged me down from the luggage rack. Annakutty screamed that I was a woman to make him stop. I understood in hindsight that there was nothing else that Annakutty could have done in that moment of panic to protect me. But at the time, I didn't know what was more humiliating, to be dragged down the way I was, or to be called a woman.

This experience along with many others, made it clear that even without surgery and hormones, there were some public spaces I could not occupy without being at the receiving end of violence. So, for a lot of us, who have socially lived as men before we even knew of the possibility of gender affirming surgeries, it is more about the intense discomfort we feel in our own bodies than the idea of how you see us. And because these surgeries are performed by plastic surgeons, it makes others believe that these surgeries are optional when in fact they are an integral part of the right to life of trans people. For those of us who desire surgery, it is not a brave choice, it is most often, the only choice.

At the end of our trip, we had seen some non committal surgeons who wanted to make money, one sleazy surgeon, an experienced surgeon, one good endocrinologist and one good psychiatrist. Among them, there was only one woman. The rates quoted by all surgeons were on the higher side of ₹50,000. My experience of having been sexually abused when I was 16 years old by a doctor during a minor surgery, made me pick the woman surgeon. It was at her office that I was waiting.

The secretary, Meena called me in. Dr Neeta smiled as we walked in. She slipped between 'she' and 'he' as she talked about me during the consultation. In my desperation to get the surgery done, I smiled weakly through a conversation that would have, in any other circumstances made me bare my fangs. She explained how the surgery would be done.

'Each patient is a signature for me. You will have minimal scarring and be able to live as a man after this. Don't worry,' she assured me.

My mother looked worried. I realized that this whole thing had just become real for her at that moment. All those years I refused to wear those frocks she stitched, the one week I cried and refused to go to school when I first menstruated, my regular visits to the barbershop as I was growing up. It all led us to this one truth—her baby was a boy then and now a man.

By the time I had fixed this appointment with the surgeon in Bombay, I had been on hormones for a little over a year. The first amongst the trans men I loved dearly to go on hormones was Deepak (though he was supposed to be part of this book, his interview recordings were not audible and Revathi had no option but to drop his story). He was a great singer and storyteller, a handsome charmer and had a great sense of humour. After facing huge struggles as a trans man who faced gender and caste violence, he ran away from home with a lover.

After years, he was able to access hormone replacement therapy, not very far from where he lived. He was just sprouting an enviable moustache when we lost him. He jumped off a train and ended his life. We were and still are, broken by how we left us. It was a brutal reminder of the fragile edge that some of our lives are lived at and reminded us of the need to support each other more, especially the ones who face multiple oppressions. Now, we crowd around the bed of a person undergoing surgery almost like emperor penguins in the Antarctic do to keep each other warm in the cold!

For accessing hormone treatment, they require your mental health to be 'assessed' and for two psychiatrists to certify you as having gender identity dysphoria (a lot of psychiatrists still write 'gender identity disorder'). Depending on your psychiatrist, this could take any amount of time, in some cases, even years. We are left at the mercy of doctors who know very little about us. In most cases, they try to convince us that we should continue to live in the same bodies, they warn us about the consequences of 'sex change'. Among trans friends,I have heard of instances of electro shock therapies, house arrests, being chained to their bed posts, trans men being forcefully administered female hormones and marriage being prescribed as a 'cure'. With no way to opt out of this oppressive medical system, I let them certify me as having a disorder. In fact, I pleaded with them to certify me, in order to become who I am today.

One of my major anxieties when I got onto hormones, was how my mother would react to my physical changes. I started looking more like the man she disliked from her past. Would she begin to see him in me more? I realized over time that she didn't hate him as much as I thought she did. It was an impossible relationship due to many reasons, some within their control and some, outside of it.

As I masculinise over the years, I have come to realize that I have also become the child who cannot be 'explained' to many. When you medically transition, the joke is over. The child can no longer be indulged as a tomboy, the 'daughter' will never get married and give you chubby grandchildren, you stumble when you say your kid's name, when you use pronouns, slowly you avoid conversations about that child with friends and family, you panic when someone rings the bell when your child is at home, you cannot ask extended circles to open a few doors of opportunity for your kid. Your erasure is written into family histories as blank spaces where your photograph once was. As someone who is convinced about the need to destroy caste networks, this erasure came as a relief to me. I have begun to understand the erasure as something that is propelled by caste respectability and shame. It must also be said that it is natural for people close to us to feel a sense of loss, to not know how to transition themselves. Once when I went home, I found my school uniform neatly folded up in my mother's cupboard. I realized then, that even as she struggled to embrace the son I had become to her, she still mourned the loss of the daughter she once thought she had given birth to. I acknowledge the incredible support I have received over time from my loved ones in this journey.

My surgery date was given. 23rd November. The surgery was to happen in a tiny operation theatre behind Dr Neeta's clinic. I arrived in the morning around 9 am and was made to change into a medical gown. I waited for two hours, trembling with fear and excitement before the anaesthetist came. The doctor came and did markings on my chest for the surgery. I was on the operation table. The last thing I remember was the colour of the nail polish on the anaesthetist's fingers. A dirty shade of green. And the glass beads on the surgeon's cap. Anaesthetised dreams I cannot recall now, followed for about 6 hours.

When I woke up it was late evening. I saw my mother through a haze. I wanted to pee badly but when I tried, I couldn't. I was taken back in an auto, to a place we had rented for 15 days. There were two plastic cans with fluids and blood on both sides of my chest. Drainage pipes. They would be removed after five days. The surgery was practically pain free and I was on the other side! I was happy. Well, almost.

I went back to remove the drains and dressings in five days. Dr Neeta removed the dressing on the left nipple and said, 'everything looks good'. Then she removed the one on the right side and said, Oh! Oh!'

Alarm bells started ringing. My heart was pounding against my newly operated chest. 'The nipple graft doesn't seem to be taking fully, but don't worry. You will be fine,' she said. I looked in the mirror. There was only blood and flesh were my nipple and areola complex should have been. She told us not to panic and sent us back. Over the next few weeks, I watched in horror as both sides of my chest opened up and became craters of flesh and blood.

Dr Neeta said, 'One other patient had the same issue. He was allergic to the sutures. We did a skin graft and he is fine'. I knew the guy she was talking about. He came with his parents to visit me and showed me his chest. She seemed to have just about fixed it with a second operation, a skin graft (Recently, I spoke to him again and learnt that he has undergone four surgeries with her since and his results are still not satisfactory!). I left Bombay on her advice that I should be back in a month for a second operation. I changed my dressings every day and waited for a month to pass.

Right before I went for the second surgery, I saw an angel kneel before Mother Mary and pray for me. It gave me hope at a time when I most needed it. That image is etched in my memory as one of unconditional love and faith.

After exactly a month, I went back for the second surgery. Same routine. Except this time I was not excited. She took skin from my thigh to reconstruct my chest. I left Bombay the next day on her advice. 'This is not a major procedure. You will be fine. You can go home,' she said.

In a week, I saw my chest disintegrating again to form the same craters of flesh and blood. I lost all desire to live. All my life I had waited for that moment.

Even before I knew it was possible to transition medically, I had waited for it. Years of self hatred and bodily shame led me to this place. Years of binding so tight I could hardly breathe. I had finally convinced myself, a psychiatrist, taken hormones, looked for doctors, got my mother this far with me on my journey and I looked down at the body I had always wanted to see and saw nothing but broken dreams. Broken dreams inside a broken chest. How I wished during those times that I had a God I could believe in, complain to, blame, be angry with!

The next few months, as I plunged into the depths of despair, defeated by my body, Dr Neeta stopped picking up my calls. She stopped responding to my messages and mails. I realized that I had been taken for a ride by a doctor who had no idea what she was doing. A doctor who was propelled more by her greed to make money than providing health care. Over the next few months, I got in touch with all the men who had gone to her for surgery and learnt that many had complications. They do not want to tell their story. And understandably so.

Soon after my experience, I put out a warning for trans men about this doctor. Let this story also be one such warning to more men who come after me. I do not for a second regret the decision to undergo the surgery, I only regret the surgeon I went to. Since then, better and cheaper resources for trans men have been located. Last month, I am happy to say, the sixth man from our close circle in Bangalore successfully underwent an affordable operation at Victoria hospital. All men except for one out of the six are from historically oppressed castes (two of those men are part of this book). All are working class men who left their families when they were young. I am convinced that before we leave this world, things will be better for younger men who come after us. We will work hard to make sure they are.

Since the beginning of time, each oppressed group has emerged in history to assert itself by recording their own valiant histories. On the walls of caves, in books, in songs, on the barks of trees, in oral traditions. Each brother who has shared his story in this book, is, as you can see, an indomitable man. Inspired by these men who have faced formidable challenges due to caste and gender, I offer this experience of mine which is nothing but a whisper in our long struggle for freedom.

A little over a year after my surgery and a relationship later, I tell this story because it is not a unique one. It is the story of many trans men and women across caste and how our bodily vulnerabilities are exploited by doctors. There is a continuum in the way doctors have dehumanised me from Dr Timothy who abused me as a 16-year old and claimed he didn't know 'it was a girl' to Dr Neeta who experimented on my body and made money off of it. It's a fact that because of my able bodied privileges I could undergo this transition, an option not available to some of my brothers who live with disabilities. This able bodied privilege also overlaps with caste privilege because I was not malnourished as a baby (malnutrition and lack of access to healthcare as a baby being one of the most prominent reasons for developmental issues leading to disabilities). It is a fact that caste and class privileges ensured that I could afford this surgery (however botched it was), take months off to heal, live with my non dependent mother, have her look after me.

For most of my brothers, this kind of support is non existent. Health care (or the lack of it) is one glaring example of how trans people across caste along with the millions of poor dalits, Muslims and adivasis of this subcontinent are denied basic rights. And so, every time a speeding ambulance goes past me on the streets, I relive my worst nightmare—of being in an accident and taken to a hospital on time, unconscious, with nobody to 'explain' why my body looks the way it does.

As stubborn skin grows over old and new wounds, I learn to love myself and give of that love to the world. I am grateful for the angel who came to me in my most desperate times, made me defy death and embraced me in her arms. I am grateful for my chosen trans family, especially my beautiful sister Smiley, who gives me courage everyday to own my scars. For making me realize that each scar has a story to tell. A story of survival and truth. And to never forget the lesson in faith I learnt from two-year old Danny boy who gave me his heart in closed baby fists, I named myself Imaan.

Gee Imaan Semmalar is a theatre actor, writer and filmmaker and co-founded Panmai Theatre, Chennai.

18

*Where are all the f2ms?**
Trans Visibility and Organizing
in India

The following piece was written in the year 2004. We are in 2016 now.

Even though most of what happened 12 years ago, belonged to that time and context, much of it lingers on.

Please read what follows with this in mind.

I address this to all those who are worrying about the lack of visibility and organizing of transgender people living in India. This is specifically about non-hijra transgendered persons. I share below briefly:

My personal process as a 32-year-old, post-operated, Indian, female to male trans person; my attempts at female to male/transgender visibility, seeking support from existing Indian queer groups, their responses and gestures; and issues that arise out of these events and experiences: my queries and fears.

---

* f2ms: female to male trans persons

My personal process as a 32-year-old post operated, Indian, female to male trans person

1976–77/: Four to five years old/playschool:

My first memory: I want to grow up to have the long sideburns my father has.

13 years old/seventh class: My girlfriend has heard of the possibility of 'sex change.' I laugh.

16 years old/tenth class: My parents find me and my girlfriend necking. I am called a lesbian; told that I should be taken to a psychiatrist, as this is an abnormality. I say that I am not abnormal. That I know I am not a lesbian. And that I don't know what/ who I am.

19 years old/first year, college: I begin my search. I go through abnormal psychology textbooks at the Dixit Library of the All India Institute Of Medical Sciences (AIIMS), New Delhi. I see the word 'Transsexual' listed in the DSM (Diagnostic and Statistical Manual of Mental Disorders,) document. I have found the word that I know names me.

1991–1997: I do research for six years. Meet surgeons and psychiatrists I have lost count of. Between 1995 and 1997, I have been assessed by two independent psychiatrists. Neither can give me leads to any other female to male person. They claim to have assessed some who don't want to be contacted. I begin talking to my parents. The parent, who once called me a lesbian, now calls me a 'hijra.' I begin talking to extended family, to my lover, to professional colleagues.

1997/26 years old/working: I start hormone therapy at AIIMS. This is their first female to male case. I get to know about a queer space for the first time. I go to one of its meets. It is a gay support group—Humrahi, at the Naz Foundation (India) Trust in Delhi.

27 years old/working: I share my research with the surgeon at AIIMS. We decide on the surgical approach. I have top surgery (mastectomy; chest surgery). This is their first f2m surgery.

28 years old/working: I meet the first other trans-identified person who wants to undergo sex reassignment. I begin the process of getting my gender identity legally changed.

Present/32 years old/professional college: Since my own reassignment, I have till date met 12 trans-identified persons living in India. Recently, I have initiated a yahoo group for transgender persons, transsexuals and intersexuals of Asian/diasporic origin. (sampoorna@yahoogroups.com)

My attempts at female to male/transgender visibility; seeking support from existing queer groups, responses and gestures

Naz Foundation, (India) Trust: In 1998–99, while undergoing sex reassignment, I was interested to start a space for transgender persons in Delhi. I approached the Naz Foundation, (India) Trust but their infrastructure was already blocked with existing groups/commitments. Ms Anjali Gopalan, however, extended access to their Internet facility to start collating information, which I was to co-ordinate with the project officer-in-charge. In spite of repeated phone calls and numerous visits where I was kept waiting endlessly, the project officer made it impossible for me to undertake the research work. Finally, I gave up.

Sangini/TARSHI: Subsequently I approached Sangini, the queer women's support group then with Naz (India). They did not feel ready for transgender persons to be part of the group. However, I started receiving phone calls from trans persons/those considering reassignment, forwarded by Sangini and another Delhi organization TARSHI (Talking About Reproductive and Sexual Health Issues). A couple of years later, Sangini invited me to hold information sessions for both their key persons and group members. Apparently, they have since opened up their space to transgender women, but only those who have sexually reassigned.

Sampoorna: From the many referrals by Sangini and Tarshi, there are three persons (two female to male trans persons and one male to female trans person) who have actively pursued their desires for transition. Together with them I have formed a network in Delhi. We have been interacting and supporting each other and those who get in touch with us on various fronts. This has been a journey of some years together since the entire process of transition is a long drawn-out one and involves all kinds of undertakings from informational, emotional, financial, legal, medical, physical, social and family support. My parents have also become a part of this network, benefiting parents of other group members. Three of us are listed in the Humjinsi Book, with our permissions, under the group name 'Sampoorn.'

Humsafar Trust: I think it was in 2002 when Mr Ashok Row Kavi mentioned to me telephonically about setting up a board and wanting a trans person on it. I asked him to write the details to me but have not heard from him again.

Aaj Tak: Around this time, as I recall, Ms Rukmini Sen, from the queer community, working with Aaj Tak, wanted me to feature on television. I was not at all clear as to what this 'visibility' would do? For whom? And on whose terms? I declined.

Lawyers Collective: Mr Alok Gupta interviewed me for the article 'Transgender, law and civil rights' for the magazine, THE LAWYERS, published by the Lawyers Collective. On the request of Mr. Vivek Diwan from the Collective, I have shared with him affidavits submitted for the legal change of my gender identity. Currently I am also mediating between a TG person and Lawyers Collective on the request of the former who wishes to enter into a legal contract of marriage.

Combat Law: Ms Ashwini Sukhtankar interviewed me for the article 'Complicating Gender: Rights Of Transsexuals In India' for the Combat Law issue: Vol.2 Issue 4/October-November, 2003.

Ms Venu Arora: This documentary filmmaker, a co-student attending the course at the Sexuality Institute organized by TARSHI and CREA (Creating Resources For Empowerment In Action), in Pune, during March,

2004, asked for email ids of other trans sexual persons I knew. I asked for a written statement ensuring confidentiality and her specific queries. I haven't heard from her yet.

Aanchal Trust: At the 2nd International Conference Of Masculinities, Sexualities and Cultures, Bangalore, June 2004, I put up a photographic Exhibition titled: 'Miscellaneous-Daily Masculinities'. Ms Geeta Kumana, from Aanchal Trust had serious issues with one of the exhibits titled 'Packing', a photographic narrative on the dildo. In fact her issue was with one particular photograph out of a series of five of this narrative. In this photograph the dildo is in the palm, held close to the primary genital area. She commented to the effect that:

'You are violating me by publicly displaying the photograph of a phallus. It is like flaunting the phallus in my face. Any ordinary Indian woman will have the response I am having.'

While, on the one hand Ms Kumana's response to the dildo narrative illustrates a complete lack of a trans perspective, on the other, in a response to Raj Joshi's email of 5th July 2004, on the lgbt-india e-list, she invites female to male trans persons to join the Aanchal Trust. Such an invitation appears to be mere tokenism.

Sangama: July 2004, Sangama Office, Bengaluru.

Kokila, a hijra person, was gang raped by ten men and later tortured by the police. I got involved on day one. During the FIR, Mr E Manohar, head of Sangama, outs me and another trans-identified person working in his office, to the investigating Lady Police Officer, without our permission. I withdraw my active support and participate from outside. Before my leaving Bengaluru, Mr E Manohar extends the following invitation:

'Come some time again. Let this (Kokila's case) die down. We will see then, what can be done about female to male trans persons.'

The tokenism never seems to end.

Issues that arise out of the above events and experiences: My queries and fears

On Organizing: Ground Realities:

Female to male trans persons and male to female trans persons are two very specific and statistically small groups within the larger one of 'transgender people.' In fact, the former are in even a greater minority when compared to the latter. By transgender people here, I mean, all persons who are gender transgressing and whose gender expression does not fit into the binary of man/woman-male/female.

Sex reassignment surgery (SRS) is a complicated, time consuming and expensive process. The medical community in India is just beginning to undertake it in a professional and accountable manner. All the surgeries (except one) of members of our group were performed in Delhi and conducted under international guidelines. Persons undergoing SRS must take responsibility for the person they choose for their surgery. If the person goes to a knife-happy surgeon, the person will get what a knife-happy surgeon can deliver. The belief that any cosmetic surgeon can perform these surgeries is completely unfounded. These are highly specialized surgeries that have to be coordinated across medical departments of gynaecology, andrology, cosmetic and reconstructive surgery and endocrinology.

It is imperative to state here that contrary to another misinformation circulating within the lgbt community in India, and in particular in reference to communications over this e-list in recent days, I think I can say on behalf of all four members of Sampoorna (this email is being forwarded to the other three), that

None of us regrets any of the surgery/interventions that we have undertaken

We are happy for the decisions that we have taken with regard to reassignment. Perhaps it is a matter of time, and much more, before we have the organized numbers to ask our rights from law, from medicine, from professional organizations, from families, from lovers.

There are lessons for us to learn from the history of LGBT organizing the world over. There are identities, which get left out or subsumed by the existing queer spaces. For example, the presence of trans-identified female bodied persons in lesbian spaces. Trans needs have not been met, even recognized, in such spaces. Prevalent lesbian notions of ways of being are inadequate for trans needs. These notions do not enable/empower the trans-identified members of lesbian spaces. Another example would be the ongoing debate about who is the 'koti'? (a male bodied person with female gender identity) The 'koti' is being understood as the 'vernacular gay-identified person' where as 'she' is clearly a transgender person.

Tied up with gender identity and expression are issues of class. Female-bodied transgender persons, specifically those who desire but cannot economically/ otherwise afford part or the whole gamut of reassignment, are the ones really being left out in the whole discourse/activism on sexuality and gender.

In addition, the intimacies of social and cultural relationships that create and nurture personhood are being taken away from trans persons. We are losing lovers for not being man-enough or woman-enough, both in straight and queer relationships. Recently a trans person was threatened by his lover's siblings. Another is being hassled for property; he is now a threat to the male-born child of his parents. Yet another is being forced into marriage as a 'cure'. The documentation of non-hijra transgendered lives in India is yet to begin.

To say that female to male trans persons are hardly visible/organized is unfair without understanding what such visibility and organizing means and what it would take. When existing queer support spaces don't have any trans perspective, when the medical community is still being located and educated, when law is still being dealt with, when dealing with family and friends is still being undertaken, it will take time and a lot more before meaningful coming together can happen.

Visibility: Where are the transgender people? Where are the female to male trans persons?

'How come you don't see disabled people in spaces that you are in? It is not that they don't exist! It's that they can't get to where you are!'

This was shared by a teacher at the earlier mentioned Sexuality Institute, on the subject of 'Disability and Sexuality'.

Where are the transgender people? Where are the female to male trans persons? It is not that they don't exist. Why are transgender people and female to male trans persons hardly seen in existing queer spaces? Why are they invisible even when they are there? Something about these spaces is not giving them what they need. What could this be?

The conceptual foundations of most of the queer spaces in India are built on a sexual identity primarily determined by the sex of the one who is desired. This constructs the identity of being gay, of being lesbian.

What then constructs the identity of a transgender? It is an identity of self. It is an identity of gender. Most of the existing queer spaces in India are not addressing gender. They are primarily focused on sexual orientation.

Trans persons are not finding any meaningful space within existing queer/LGBT groups. These have in fact been and are increasingly being trans-unfriendly; even trans-phobic. Two days ago, I was told by a trans person, who belongs to a lesbian support group, what the key person there said to him:

'The day you reassign, you count yourself out of the group.'

Yet another lesbian support group asks male to female trans persons to cross-dress to prove their credentials for claiming membership. In January, 2004, at the World Social Forum, Mumbai, I was asked to leave a meeting, the topic of which was 'Lesbian Torture' even after some of my lesbian friends there introduced me as a post-operated female to male trans person.

One of our critiques of hetero patriarchy has been that it has constructed and enforced only two genders.

How are we doing any better when we too ask for the same gender conformity within existing queer spaces?! And what of those who do not want to reassign? Of those who want to but can't, either due to money or disability or other health concerns or even social reasons? Or those who want to reassign partially? What about intersexuals? And what about transgender people/transsexuals/intersexuals who are gay/lesbian/bisexual/pansexual?

Where is the 't' in L.G.B.T?

Satya Rai Nagpaul is a national award winning cinematographer. A graduate from the Film & Television Institute of India [FTII], his filmography includes the feature films Aligarh, Chauthi Koot, Zinda Bhaag, Gattu *and* Anhey Ghode Da Daan. *He is a trans man and a gender activist. He founded Sampoorna, a network of trans* and intersex Indians, which has been running since the early 2000s. In 2010, he was elected to the India Task Force of SAHRA, the South Asian Association for the Rights of Marginalized Genders and Sexualities. In 2014, he co-led the first South Asian Trans masculine, Intersex and Intergender meet, conducted in eight languages with 40 participants. In 2016, he was the trans masculine nomination to head the National TG Task Force, constituted to work with the Inter Ministerial Committee [IMC] for the implementation of the NALSA judgment.*

19

I Have a Dream

For the past 20 years, a significant number of well-funded NGOs have been working in the HIV/AIDS sector in India. For 20 years they have been talking only about condoms, safe sex and preventing AIDS. But as you have seen from my story and the stories of so many other trans people, we are dealing with many more complex issues than just AIDS. We are dealing with state violence, lack of trans health care, public violence, sexual abuse and lack of acceptance from families, to name just a few. We have not even begun talking about acceptance for trans people. Nobody can estimate how much money has been spent on this HIV activism. I am sure the figures are staggering.

According to me, they could have given some of that money to trans people and built houses for them. That would have been more useful work. So many of our people are dying of poverty on the streets. Even persons from the trans community who are recruited in NGOs often work against their own people. Beyond a point, I don't blame them. They are looking after their own livelihoods. My question is: what have the NGOs done to improve the lives of street based hijras who are harassed by the police every day?

I also worked in an NGO once. I thought then that I was working to improve the lives of people in my community. Back then, they would fly me out to Delhi and other places to talk. Now that I have quit the NGO sector, they don't invite me for anything. In fact, they are so scared of critical voices, they will silence you before you can talk. The first Hijra Habba was organized by Famila along with her sisters. They raised funds for the programme by begging on the streets. Now many funded NGO projects are using the same title for events but do not remember or acknowledge Famila and the fact that it was first started by her. If people who claim to work for trans people behave like this, what is to be expected of others? If they get funding for another ten years they will continue to do the same thing.

From Delhi to Tamil Nadu, most NGOs prepare reports even before they hold the meetings for which they are supposed to do them, and they ensure just a token presence—if at all—of trans people. Everything is done according to their needs and their funders' needs. They book big rooms in hotels and talk about street-based hijras without their presence. They waste so much food at their buffets but talk about poverty and starvation. Over time, I learnt to be critical of their role in our communities.

I go to universities now to talk about trans people, but when they say they will get me flight tickets, I say that I will come by train and if they give me the money instead, I can eat for two months. But they don't even give me consultation fees. But now, I notice that they don't invite me as much, maybe because I am critical of NGOs and no longer employed by them.

The main issue is really that trans people lack employment options. Trans women are provided with just two options--begging and sex work. Trans men, however, even if educated, find it difficult to get mainstream jobs because their legal gender and names read differently on their papers. Most of the female to male trans persons I know work as drivers, run or work in small businesses and try to be self-employed in some way or the other, or they work in NGOs.

Everyone says we are lazy. The public, the law and the police say that we beg because we are lazy and won't take up opportunities even if we are given options. But my request to them is, please give us the options and then see what we can do. People are scared of us and do not rent their houses to us. They think we are immoral, we drink, steal and have every possible vice. My heartfelt appeal is not to criminalize us and brand us as having every possible vice just because we are hijras.

I turn and ask them, politicians are looting the people and the nation and putting all their money in foreign banks. We are not doing bigger wrongs than them, right? For instance, there is armed robbery of banks. Don't you know about such things or are you not bothered by this? You drive away adivasis and give away the minerals to big companies. You drive away people in slums and give the land to big builders. You drive away beggars and put them in places like the beggar's colony. Is our wrongdoing worse than all these violations?

Some people ask us to give up begging first. They say our lives will then be better. There are beggars in all communities. But you think none of us has dignity. Think about why we beg when you ask us to give up begging. Today, without any support, we stand alone and fight. Does anyone give us food, clothing or funding for our fight? How many of you have raised your voices for our rights? To struggle on these streets, only by begging can I feed and clothe myself.

Take for instance, Swapna who was born in Madurai. The Tamil Nadu Public Service Commission rejected her candidature due to her gender status. She went to court for her rights and the court gave a positive judgment. She then wrote the exam and qualified for Grade 4. She wishes to be an IAS officer. In between this, she has to feed herself, she goes to a company for work, and her SSLC certificate is in her given, male name. She faces a lot of trouble because of this discrepancy. She gave an application to the Education Department to change this. They said they could change the name, but not the gender. She went to court. Then the court said okay to the gender change. But the Education Department has not made the change so far. So to take up employment, see the difficulties we have to face!

Yalini, a sub-inspector in Salem, faced a similar problem. Now she's got a court order and she has been able to write her exam. Grace Banu, who has faced caste and gender violence, is studying engineering now after overcoming all these difficulties. Living Smile Vidya has also got a Masters Degree in linguistics and she went to London to study theatre. A lot of them also face caste oppression. None of these women gets support or lakhs of rupees worth of funding from NGOs. The hijra jamaat does not support them. They have come up independently and are role models for our communities. The time for clapping hands and begging for money has gone, but the time for clapping hands and begging for education is here. The government says that everyone should have the right to education. What do you say to this then? People in power try everything to not implement SC/ST reservation in education. With us, they don't even have to try because not even one door is open for us anyway. Let me ask the people who ask us to give up begging, do your kids struggle for education like this?

Look at the Shilpa case of 2008 (referred to earlier) in which Mangala, her guru, was released after two years. Now, they say that she was wrongfully imprisoned. They say now that Shilpa was 18 years old and voluntarily underwent surgery but then why was she caught and taken to a well-known corporate by her parents and the police? Why did they forcibly make her undergo a phalloplasty? She still lives with trans people now. She still is a trans woman, so what punishment will you give the police and doctor then? Mangala was in jail for two and a half years for helping Shilpa live in her chosen gender. What compensation will you give for the loss of so many years of her life? For all the torture she went through?

Justice KS Radhakrishnan Panicker and Justice AK Sikri delivered a Supreme Court judgment on April 15, 2014 popularly called the NALSA judgment. The NALSA judgment has given the option of third gender status to trans people. It says that all trans persons whether hijra, trans woman, trans man can self identify as man, female, transgender without surgical interventions and hormones. But a lot of newspapers reported that it is a third gender judgment. I don't think of myself as the third gender. By giving this recognition, the courts have ushered in a new kind of discrimination. See for instance, the newspaper report of a trans woman Amruta Soni, whose visa to attend a health conference in the US was kept on hold because she had T as sex on her passport. So, does the state give us this third gender recognition only to discriminate against us further?

They say LGBT people have 'unnatural sex'. What is meant by 'natural sex'? If the objective is reproduction, the sex is termed legal. For contraception and for safer sex condoms were popularized. So is that sex unnatural? So is any sex that is not for reproduction unnatural? Is there only penile vaginal sex between a husband and wife?

Sec 377 of IPC is used against homosexuals and they highlight this in the news. But it is also against animal sex, non-penile vaginal sex between husband wife, sex with minors and sex with animals. Why are the NGOs or newspapers not talking about this? They have made the myth that IPC sec 377 is about homosexuality and in effect made homosexuals into criminals by reiterating it. Many newspapers ask me about homosexuality. I am a heterosexual trans woman. I only speak in solidarity with homosexuals. People, especially journalists, don't have the smallest idea how to ask questions sensitively and report intelligently.

It is not wrong for one person to love another, even if that love is of any gender. The British who introduced Section 377, left this land many years back. They don't have this law in their own countries but we are stubbornly clinging on to it. Is there any meaning in upholding such a law now? You describe earthquakes, tsunamis and cyclones as natural disasters. But this unnatural love doesn't destroy anyone, does it?

Do not see homosexuals and trans women as mere sex objects. We also have feelings of love. Some of us want to become parents. All of us want live with dignity.

If Famila were alive today, several lesbians and female to male trans persons would have got support from her. Many claim to work for trans people. But even in feminist groups they only talk about lesbians. But female to male trans persons do not get jobs in their offices though they all claim to be progressive. I have found that what they say is different and what they practice is different.

The loss of Famila is not just my loss because she was my daughter but it is a loss for the entire community. People driven by jealousy tried to pull her down from rising to fame and she was made to quit her job. Today so many NGOs speak about sex work as a right and they take money for projects to do with this, but then if someone in the office does sex work, the male heads get together and say that she should not do so. Today they want unions to talk about this; they discriminated against Famila and asked her to choose one job, but they did not pay her enough to run her house. I leant so much from Famila—my politics, my compassion for female to male trans persons, and maturity in my relationships. It was not a conventional guru-chela relationship at all. I learnt and took from her as much as I taught and gave her. I still miss her very deeply after all these years. We have worked on these issues for so many years and yet we could not keep Famila alive.

We could not support someone like Swapna in her education. So many of our children are killing themselves, so many of them are living on the streets, so many of them are being driven out of their homes.

My main point is that parents need to be convinced first. If they accept that their children are different, then a lot of these issues can be solved. Today, after the NALSA judgment, they say that trans people can apply to universities. But can someone like me who has failed to complete schooling apply for this? Why don't you bring awareness in schools or ensure anti-discrimination in schools first?

When we did a play on my life in a primary school in Karnataka, the kids watched with interest. However, when a scene that enacted sexual violence in my life was shown, the teachers got agitated and wanted to stop the play. Teachers themselves do not have any awareness of these issues. They skip even the reproductive lessons in biology class. I feel these issues should be taught to students at least from the 9th class. If this had been done 20 years back, at least some of the trans people who are on the streets might not be. According to me the most important things are: one, parents and their acceptance of who we are and two, introducing these issues in school so we are not demonized and made to drop out. At least the NALSA judgment should be implemented in this manner.

If my parents had accepted me, I wouldn't have left my home and come out and lived on the streets, and I would not have had to face violence from the police and goondas. I would have recognized who I was if we had learnt about trans people in school. People would have recognized me too as natural.

All legal changes have to be done by the state. These changes should be done quickly so that we don't spend half our lives running after different state departments for them. I would also have got a well paid job somewhere if all this had happened. Swapna and Banu have faced this and still fighting for this in Tamil Nadu.

Surely, if NGOs and activists work on these issues, we will see some changes. It is for the affected communities to decide what needs to be done. In many meetings, people ask about female to male trans persons. Do they exist? Is their population small? You see us hijras on the roads; you don't see the trans men. They cannot come out of their homes when they are young so easily because they are born female. Many of them are forcibly married when young. Even if they escape this, if they leave home and dress in men's clothes, people don't accept them as men. They don't get jobs so easily. They are asked to come in female clothes. Even if they are good at their work, they are judged by their appearance. If they are found out, they face a lot of sexual abuse. Even in this HIV sector, nobody works for them. Forget the NGOs, even my hijra community doesn't accept them. As the lives of my many trans men sons show, people are reluctant to accept them as men. They ask, 'how can we accept such persons as men?' Hijras say, 'Ask them to come out, talk to the media. We've also done that, have we not?'

Do you know how many problems they face when they come out? Trans man Kiran and his partner spoke to the media and were attacked with stones and chappals. Because our society is so patriarchal, I feel that even some of us who are women are unable to understand their situation. Their discrimination started in the womb, because they are born as women, and they have become men. Through my daughter Famila, I got to learn about them. I have many sons now and that's a blessing.

The term transgender, I want you to acknowledge, also includes female to male trans people. They might not come on the road or speak to the media. At least if we accept them as sons or brothers in trans communities, they will have a family. That is what Famila wanted and that is precisely what I want. It is not necessary to give birth to become a mother. When they call me 'amma', I accept them. Because I am a mother to them, I take them along with me on my journey. This is only a small step. My wish is that at least those who read this should understand and accept them. Today, in India, many female to male trans people work as drivers and construction workers, some even run bakeries. They all live as men. We do not see them. We do not know about them. You cannot say that we hijras are more in number or that they are fewer. You cannot say we are more discriminated against than they are. Many of their problems are not known to us. We cannot even imagine them. I have been able to understand a few of their issues through my long-standing association with them. I have collected the stories of about ten people but I have included only a few of trans men (five stories that I transcribed based on interviews and two stories written by trans men) in this book. This is only a seed for promoting the self-expressions of my sons. I hope that many of them will be encouraged to write their personal stories to create awareness.

The gang rape of a young woman in Delhi on December 16, 2012, created national and international headlines. I certainly don't condone the heinous crime. But sexual violence against gender non-conforming children takes place as a matter of routine. Does the media ever bother to highlight this? Which activist has taken this issue up? Has the government even bothered to acknowledge this? It is widely known that a man can sexually violate a girl or a woman. But few people are even aware that a man can and usually violates children who are gender non-conforming. Sadly, this is a non-issue.

When I was sexually abused as a child, I felt powerless and extremely vulnerable. I thought I deserved it because I had done something wrong. I was ashamed of myself for being 'different'—for wanting to play five stones, kho kho and skipping with girls when boys of my age played volleyball and kabbadi. Because I am doing something 'wrong,' the teacher pinches my thighs and touches parts of my body, which I don't like.

What is the reason for the secrecy, shame and silence surrounding the lives of the transgender community? Today some aspects of our lives are in the public domain because we transgender individuals have launched a struggle for our right to a life of dignity and respect. There have been no interventions on the part of education, health care and law to address our needs and concerns. I raise these issues because as a member of the affected community I have undergone needless pain and turmoil.

Some of you might say that unless we come out in the open about our problems, how will others know what we go through? But according to me, society has failed in its duty towards us. How was it that you overlooked us? Perhaps it was the convenient thing to do. Then how is it that you notice that we are into street based sex work and begging –professions that are criminalized in your eyes. And then you make a hue and cry about us being a disgrace to society!

The legend of Aravan, the son of Arjuna in the *Mahabharata* is well known. Equally well known is the half-man, half-woman representation of Ardhanariswara. If God assumes a gender variant form, you worship and venerate him/her. But if one of your own is a transgender person, you consider us aliens.

Finally, I look forward to a world where there is no gender at all. I don't feel like a third gender. I feel like a woman. I feel there will be more discrimination because of this 'third gender' status. How many toilets will you make for all of our genders? Trans people change to male or female according to how they feel. Hence we can use the same toilets as everyone else. What is more important, I feel, is housing, education, legal gender changes and other matters that have practical implications in our everyday lives. By overcoming and destroying caste, religion, gender, colour, and hierarchies, everyone should be able to see humans as humans. Accept us as humans. Respect our desire to live our lives with dignity and respect. Like you or anyone else. That's all I ask of you as readers of this book.

I have a dream. Perhaps over the years there will be a gradual erasure and eventual disappearance of stigma and discrimination. My life has been a striving towards making this dream a reality for all my trans sisters, daughters and sons.

20

The Supreme Court Judgment

On April 15, 2014, the Supreme Court (SC) of India passed a landmark judgment[1] that created the option of third gender status for hijras or transgender people. The SC asked the Centre to treat transgender people as socially and economically backward. According to a Supreme Court directive, being formally recognized and accorded special status, transgender people will henceforth be considered as OBCs (Other Backward Castes). They will be given reservation as OBCs. The apex court said that transgender people would be allowed admission in educational institutions and given employment on the basis that they belong to the third gender category.

The Supreme Court said that the absence of law recognizing hijras as third gender people could not continue to be used to deny them equal opportunities in education and employment. It upheld the constitutional rights of trans people as equal citizens of the country. The apex court also said that the states

---

[1] supremecourt*ofindia.nic.in/outtoday/wc40012.pdf*. Accessed on July 14, 2015.

and the Centre would have to devise social welfare schemes for the transgender community and run a public awareness campaign to address social stigma.

The judgment adopted a humane and compassionate view of the widespread stigma and discrimination experienced by members of the transgender community. Describing us as individuals whose[2] 'mind and body disowned their biological sex', transgender persons have been ostracized and ridiculed by society. But the '... moral failure lies in society's unwillingness to embrace different gender identity and expressions, a mindset which we have to change.'

According to the judgment, non-recognition our gender identity violates Articles 14 and 21 of the Constitution of India, which accords fundamental equality to all citizens.

In 2012 NALSA (National Legal Services Authority), constituted in 1997 under the provision of the Legal Services Authority Act, to provide legal services free of charge to women and marginalized communities, filed a writ petition seeking to redress the multiple discriminations experienced by the transgender community. NALSA filed a social interest litigation on providing third gender status to hijras, on reservation and other issues. Laxmi Narayan Tripathi, a transgender rights activist from Mumbai intervened in this case with the help of lawyer Anand Grover (project director of HIV/AIDS unit of Lawyers Collective in Delhi).

It was argued that transgender people are not treated as either male or female, nor are we given the status of a third gender, and hence we are being deprived of

[2] Ibid

many of the rights and privileges which other persons enjoy as citizens of this country. Transgender people are deprived of social and cultural participation and hence their access to education, health care and public places is restricted. This deprives them of the Constitutional guarantee of equality before the law and equal protection from laws.

An important aspect of the judgment is that the right to choose one's gender identity is integral to the right to lead a life of dignity, which is guaranteed by Article 21 of the Constitution of India. Hence the judgment sought to grant transgender persons the right of choice to opt for male, female or third gender classification.

As used in the writ petition,[3] the term 'third gender is an umbrella term for persons whose gender identity, gender expression or behaviour does not conform to their biological sex. Hijras describe themselves as "third gender" and they do not identify as either male or female. Since hijras do not have reproduction capacities as either men or women, they are neither men nor women and claim to be an institutional 'third gender'. Among hijras, there are emasculated (castrated, nirvana) men, non-emasculated men (not castrated/akva/akka) and intersex persons. Transgender also includes persons who intend to undergo Sex Reassignment Surgery (SRS) or have undergone SRS to align their biological sex with their gender identity in order to become male or female. They are generally called transsexual persons.'

Though the judgment uses the derogatory word 'eunuch' and describes us in terms of lack of

3 supremecourtofindia.nic.in/outtoday/wc40012.pdf

reproductive capacity, I welcome this judgment of the Supreme Court of India, as it is unique in the history of India. I convey my heartfelt gratitude to the eminent lawyers and the NALSA team who spearheaded this initiative.

However, neither I nor the members of the transgender community have the capacity to understand every nuance of this landmark judgment. But thanks to some of my friends, I was able to understand the main points it has raised. Even before the judgment was delivered on April 15, 2014, the day was commemorated in Tamil Nadu as Transgender (Thirunangai) day. I am happy that now it is a cause for national celebration too.

Although one part of me is happy, a deep sadness and yearning lurks in some corner of my heart. I feel as if I have lost something. Although I like several aspects of the judgment, I also feel disturbed that there have been several significant omissions, the discrimination and exclusiveness in the language used, and non-recognition of the experiences, needs and concerns of trans men or female to male trans persons.

Apart from me, several of my transgender community people (that also includes trans men), have considerable reservations and confusion about the implications of the judgment. The most important question that comes to our minds is this: What is meant by the term transgender? What is meant by the term third gender? Who is included? Who is left out?

In my opinion, the judgment is based heavily on the testimonies and experiences of the HIV/AIDS sector. As we all know, targeted interventions in HIV/AIDS rest almost exclusively on male to female transgender individuals. There is confusion regarding who exactly is a transgender. They are known by different names in different parts of the country—aravani, kothi, kinnar, hijra, jogappa, and shiva shakti. The judgment talks at length about each of these groups and highlights their human rights violations.

The judgment talks about the various forms of stigma and discrimination these groups experience. It also quotes a small section from *The Truth about Me*, highlighting my experiences. Unfortunately, I have not been acknowledged and my experience has been passed off as that of another non transgender person.

However, as far as I am concerned, the term transgender includes both male to female trans persons (trans women) and also female to male trans persons (trans men). However, trans men have not even been mentioned in the judgment, except for two passing references. As a transgender activist, I am disappointed by this obvious 'invisibilization' of trans men. I would also like to make it clear that I am not opposing the judgment. At some point, the judgment indirectly refers to the experiences of trans men. But my concern is that when trans women are in the centre stage of the judgment, why have trans men been cast away in the background, unseen and unheard?

Even the media, unfortunately has not played the role of the watchdog. Not one publication, electronic or print, has questioned the blatant omission of the experiences of trans men. Instead the media celebrates it as a victory for trans women. As one person, I know I cannot change the world. On my part, every year on April 15, after the third gender judgment, several of my friends wish me on Transgender Day. I use this opportunity to create awareness among people through the social media. Who is a transgender? We need to acknowledge and validate the experiences of trans men too. We often talk of gender minorities. Trans men are a minority within an already marginalized group. It is unfair if we exclude or subsume them.

I strongly object to the use of the insensitive term 'eunuch' to describe trans women and hermaphrodites to describe intersex people. We transgender activists have been spearheading a long battle to discontinue the use of these derogatory terms. These are colonial medicalized usages. The term eunuch referred to emasculated men who were appointed to guard the king's harem when the king was away. Many of my trans women friends were hurt and distressed by this gross insensitivity.

Another question that comes to my mind is this: Is it necessary to have a separate category as the third gender? For instance, I identify myself as a woman. My trans men friends identify themselves as men. This is in accordance with the principle of self-identification in determining one's gender identity and its expression—well articulated in the judgment.

My concern is that if we have a separate box such as third gender, would it inadvertently increase the stigma and discrimination of a community that is a gender minority? For example, trans women use the women's toilets in public spaces. Once there is a legal entity called the third gender, women might object to trans women using toilets meant for them and demand that they use those specially meant for them. Even if the government constructs toilets for the third gender, trans women cannot use those meant for trans men and vice versa. Even if such gender segregated toilets are a reality, trans people will become highly visible and singled out for being 'different.' Thus the likelihood of increased stigma and discrimination is a serious threat that would make the transgender community even more vulnerable.

The Supreme Court has also directed each state to consult with the hijra community on the third gender judgment and send them their recommendations. However, until date, with the exception of some states, many, including Tamil Nadu where I live, have not sent in the recommendations based on the community level consultations that reflect their needs, concerns and priorities. Both the state and central governments are not clear about certain aspects in the judgment and have approached the Supreme Court for clarifications.

Personally, I do not believe that a court judgment can change the world. We have several instances of progressive legislation—the anti dowry bill and the 33 per cent reservation for women in municipal and village elections to cite a few examples. Yet dowry crimes and women's under representation in politics continue. Even if laws are favourable, if mindsets and attitudes that are crucial for social acceptance, do not change, we are stuck in the same groove.

The third gender judgment intends to give back our lost lives and has mandated the state and central governments to help us in this regard. Can the government restore our lost lives? Can it apply salve on my wounds? Will I get back my past life? The missed opportunities? I understand it is pointless to harp about these things now.

I would also like to mention here that the Supreme Court has rejected the judgment of the Delhi High Court that decriminalized same sex relationships. In my experience it is not only gays who are victimized by the IPC 377 but also trans women as well against whom it is misused and false cases imposed on them. Ironically the third gender judgment seeks to validate our worth as humans who have the right to a life of dignity and respect. But by rejecting the Delhi High Court judgment it severely restricts our right to sexual fulfillment and marriage. Does this mean we have to lead a life of sexual abstinence?

My prime concern is that the next generation of transgender people should not go through what I have undergone. It is only now that issues concerning the transgender community are out in the public domain. This was not so even 15-20 years back. No legislation can restore their lost lives for trans people of my generation. Can I go back to being a 12-year-old? Can I live the life I longed for? Twenty years back, I wanted to become a lawyer. Is that possible now?

But for the present and future generation of trans people, I dare to dream of an equitable and accepting world—a world in which legislation and acceptance mutually support each other. The third gender judgment has indeed accorded recognition for trans women—that we too exist and need to be regarded as humans. It is a welcome step but not sufficient to foster complete acceptance and lasting social change.

21

A Ray of Hope

As an activist, I live on hope. Despite the many challenges, I still persist. Although I often wonder if I am chasing a fading rainbow.

One such recent promising development is the Rights of Transgender Persons Bill, 2015, the first private member bill passed in the Rajya Sabha in the last 36 years, on April 24, 2015 by Mr Tiruchy Siva, Member of Parliament from DMK. In another first, it is a bill introduced by a legislator who was not acting on behalf of the executive.

On April 13, 2013, I was invited as a special speaker in the Women's Revolution Conference organized by the political party Dravida Kazhagam, in Coimbatore. I spoke about the human rights violations experienced by transgender people in their homes, at school and in society in general. I even suggested that the Tamil Nadu Aravani Welfare Board be renamed as Tamil Nadu Transgender Welfare Board and that it reach out to trans men as well. The members of the Dravida Kazhagam received my suggestions and presented them to the then chief minister of Tamil Nadu.

Today this is being taken forward by Mr Tiruchy Siva, the DMK MP from Tamil Nadu in the Rajya Sabha, who has had a long-standing involvement with transgender issues. As a transgender activist, this is a moment of deep satisfaction for me. The bill has been drafted by Anuvindha, a brilliant 21-year-old young woman, a LAMP (Legislative Assistant for Member of Parliament) Fellow, who is assisting Mr Siva. I am not surprised that several international and national NGOs are now trying to take credit for this. The Bill, to ensure equality for transgender people, was passed by a unanimous voice vote. If it is to become law, his Bill will need to be passed by the Lok Sabha and get presidential assent.

The comprehensive Rights of Transgender Persons Bill,[1] 2014, aims to formulate and implement a national policy that ensures holistic development of transgender persons and their welfare to be undertaken by the state. The most encouraging feature of the proposed bill is that it is inclusive in nature. It includes trans women but also trans men (whether or not they have undergone SRS, hormone replacement therapy, laser therapy and other allied therapies), gender queer people and several socio cultural gender identities such as kinnars, hijras, aravanis, jogtas and other such groups. The Bill rests on the following core principles of equality and dignity: non-discrimination, participation in society, equality of opportunity, accessibility and acceptance of transgender persons as part of human diversity.

The Bill has several appealing features that indicate that it has been well thought through. I'm particularly impressed by the following aspects: protection of child

[1] Archives of Srishti Madurai

rights of transgender children (especially against birth family violence), inclusive education for transgender children, adult education for transgender persons, non-discrimination in employment, social security, non-discrimination and barrier-free access in health care settings, including provision of SRS free of charge, rehabilitation programmes in health, education and employment based on comprehensive assessment of issues faced by transgender people, reservation in jobs and setting up of state and national commissions for transgender persons.

The entire transgender community is keenly waiting for the day when the bill becomes a reality. All political parties must be supportive of such initiatives—that will make all the difference to our community. When that happens, it will be the first but very important step towards a truly inclusive world—a world where there are no barriers of gender, caste, race, colour and language.

However, I must sound a note of caution. Like Babasaheb Ambedkar said, legal change without social freedom is meaningless. Even the best legislation in the world is of no use if people's mindsets and attitudes remain closed. True equality emerges only when women are treated with respect; as equals in the true sense of the term. Only when this happens, will trans people also be truly respected as humans.